The Weapon of Medjugorje

Mr. Guy Murphy O.P. (Lay Dominican)

Nihil Obstat

Reverend William Woestman,
O.M.I., J.C.D.
Censor Deputatus
January 6, 2006

Imprimatur

Bishop-elect George J. Rassas,
Vicar General
Archdiocese of Chicago
January 12, 2006

The Nihil Obstat and Imprimatur are official declarations that a book is free of doctrinal and moral error. No implication is contained therein that those who have granted the Nihil Obstat and Imprimatur agree with the content, opinions, or statements expressed. In fact, as of this date, the Church has made no official pronouncement as to the authenticity of the apparitions at Medjugorje. Those who granted the Nihil Obstat and Imprimatur do not assume any legal responsibility associated with publication.

Order this book online at www.trafford.com
or email orders@trafford.com

Most Trafford titles are also available at major online book retailers.

Printed in the United States of America.

ISBN: 978-1-4251-6304-4 (sc)
ISBN: 978-1-4251-6305-1 (e)

Trafford rev. 12/28/2010

 www.trafford.com

North America & international
toll-free: 1 888 232 4444 (USA & Canada)
phone: 250 383 6864 ◆ fax: 812 355 4082

Since our first parents ate the forbidden fruit, anxiety, confusion, hatred, and death entered the world. The whole world longs to find the antidote, the Tree of Life (Genesis 3:22) in order to have peace, clarity, true love and to live forever.

On this journey, the true Tree of Life found me and I am so happy to eat its fruit. I hope this little book helps lead you to experience this wonderful tree. (Revelations 22: 14)

DEDICATION

I dedicate this book to the Blessed Virgin Mary, the Holy Mother of God. I am eternally grateful that She took my confused soul and truly "Magnified the Lord" Jesus Christ for me. (Luke 1:46)

SPECIAL SPIRITUAL THANKS TO:

Bishop Roger Kaffer
Joseph Reinholtz
Ann Patterson
Dr. Dean Murphy
Fr. Francis Budovic

THANKSGIVING

Special thanks to the following for helping with this book:

Fr. Timothy Manley O.P.   Maria Piec
Charmaine Murphy   Monica Hammerschmidt
Charles Lawler   Garrett Fosco
The Paul Family   Larry and Mary Sue Eck
Fr. Dan Bachner   Dianne Bozak
Redd Griffin   Charnai Fankhanel
Susan Tassone   Blossom Thomas

TABLE OF CONTENTS

CHAPTER ONE - EARLY YEARS

Life can be directed by your attitude. Newton's Law of Motion includes: "If a body is in motion, it will remain in motion unless an external force acts upon it." Similarly, our lives follow a certain path; we remain on that path unless an external force acts upon us. To change the path of our life is called a conversion.

This is a true story about a double conversion, an academic and a spiritual one. In both cases, my heart viewed chemistry and religion as empty, meaningless formulas. Nothing was going to change my mind about this, or so I thought.

Growing up in Medinah, Illinois, a Chicago suburb, I was bored with school. There seemed to be so much useless information. Was the only purpose of this information to provide busy work, so that there was less time for play? I did just enough to get by. I spent a sizeable part of those years looking out the window, and my grades showed it. They reflected my attitude.

One subject I found especially frustrating and confusing was chemistry. All those C's, O's, H's, S's and K's: what did I care if some combination of these letters can change a paper's color to blue or not?

During my sophomore year in high school, a friend, I'll call "Carmen," came up with the formula to "Snap and Pops." This weak explosive sold in stores contained small "pops" wrapped in tissue paper. When one of them struck the ground, it ignited and popped. One day, Carmen and I sneaked into the Christian Brother's private lab, to make a batch of his formula. As Carmen finished filtering out the product and placed it onto a paper towel set on the floor, I thought, "There is no way this pile of mud is going to do anything." I had no faith in his formula.

As the mud dried, Carmen scooped a few particles out of the pile and put them on the floor a few inches away. He started hitting them with the end of his pencil. As they dried, we could hear faint pops. The pops increased my faith that there might be something to this formula. With our heads close to the ground to hear better, we started to snicker. As Carmen continued to scoop, some particles fell to the ground, creating an inadvertent fuse.

As he struck the powder with the back of his pencil, the pop ignited the fuse. Our eyes were fixed closely on the beauty of the burning fuse. Our heads turned to watch the flame approach the large pile. KAA-POW! The pile blew up, and we sprang to our feet. The noise was louder than a firecracker. Fear seized my heart and my left ear was ringing. With my right ear, I could hear footsteps approaching the lab. Students caught with firecrackers or other explosives would be expelled from school. I started to panic.

The footsteps stopped. A Christian Brother, named Brother Tom, shouted, "What is going on?" Carmen calmly explained how he dropped a book, and it made a loud noise. Brother Tom did not buy it for a minute. He interrogated us while he walked around the lab, looking for evidence. When the formula blew up, it spread powder all over the floor. As Brother Tom walked, Carmen and I could hear the pop, pop, pop, under his shoes. My heart started to pound. Brother Tom had a hearing aid, but even with it he couldn't hear too well. Fortunately, Brother was not aware of the convicting evidence he was looking for.

Out of the corner of my eye, I could tell that Carmen looked at me. Had I looked back, I would have burst out laughing. Due to lack of maturity, I would laugh uncontrollably over the smallest things. The fear of facing my parents after having been expelled from school and the urge to laugh were both growing, and I went into a kind of "shock." Every part of my body froze. Brother Tom got right in my face and yelled, "What are you doing in here?" Wow! What a tough question! I looked at him with a frozen face and prayed, "God, I will do whatever You say for the rest of my life, please get me out of this mess."

Brother Tom stopped his investigation, threw us out of the lab and growled, "Don't ever come in here again unless you have permission." Upon leaving, I was so stiff that I must have looked like the "Tin Man" from the "*Wizard of Oz.*"

For the next three days, I walked around with a frozen face, but inside I was reliving every detail of our lab ordeal. For the first time in my life, I realized that chemical formulas were not here just to keep us busy, they were a way of attaining power over nature. These formulas give us fuel for rockets, gasoline for cars, electricity for our homes. These formulas are real, and they make life easier. I was truly fascinated, and this fascination triggered a change of attitude. Slowly, this new attitude started to reflect in my grades. Eventually, I graduated college with high honors in chemical engineering. The burning desire to see things for myself, and to experience formulas as opposed to just writing them on paper provided the key incentive to helping me grow academically.

Looking back on my life, I realized that this one eventful day in the lab began my academic conversion.

In college, another type of conversion was taking root, a far deeper and broader one -- a conversion of my spirit. It began when I heard about miracles happening in Medjugorje, a small village in

Yugoslavia. In Medjugorje, Jesus's Mother, the Blessed Virgin Mary, was reported to have been appearing to six teenagers every day. They describe seeing a beautiful young woman about 18 to 20 years old, with a gray dress, white veil, rosy cheeks, blue eyes, long black hair, with a crown of stars around her head, and She was floating on a cloud. She said, "God exists, and He loves you. God alone is the fullness of life. If you want to enjoy that fullness and obtain peace, you must turn back to God." Our Lady was giving them many messages for the world, along with ten secrets of future events. Several miracles were actually occurring to confirm the message.

"Miracles happening today? I thought all the miracles accepted in my Roman Catholic religion had happened two thousand years ago. I have to see this for myself!" Thinking about going to Medjugorje caused me to reflect on the faith. To discern whether the visions of Medjugorje were true or not, I had to brush up on my religion. Even after eight years of Catholic grade school, four years of Catholic high school, and two years of Catholic college, I did not know one thing about the faith. Not one. Before, I did not know and I really did not care. Now I cared, but I realized I did not understand. The more I tried to learn, the less I understood. Even the simple things did not make sense. Upon analyzing the song, "The Little Drummer Boy," I could not figure out why the delicate ear of the Baby Jesus would want to hear the sharp rapping noise of a drum. Baffling!!! To clear up the confusion about religion, I decided to read the Bible.

CHAPTER TWO - READING THE BIBLE
LOOKING FOR THE TREE OF LIFE

Picking up the Bible for the first time in years opened a great fear in me. If people knew I was reading the Bible, they might think I was a fanatic. To overcome this fear, I told myself that the Bible has been the biggest selling book of all time, and I never cared in the past what people thought of me. Nevertheless, because of this fear, I read the Bible in secret for the next year.

The first stories in the Bible are fascinating. Everyone is familiar with the Garden of Eden. God gave our first parents, Adam and Eve, everything they could ever want or need in Paradise and made a covenant with them not to eat the forbidden fruit of one tree called the "Tree of Knowledge of good and evil," or they would DIE THE DEATH. (Genesis 2:17) The Devil appears as a serpent and tricks them into breaking the covenant. Adam blames both Eve and God. Eve blames the serpent. God expels them from the Garden, and the history of the human race has been a comedy and tragedy of errors ever since.

Reading Genesis, I realized that the "Tree of Knowledge of good and evil" was not the only special tree in the Garden. There was a second special tree. The other tree was called the "Tree of Life." Had Adam and Eve eaten the fruit from that tree, they would have LIVED FOREVER! (Genesis 3:22) On reading this, I literally fell out of my chair and onto the floor. "Could there be an anti-dote? How come I had never heard of this Tree before?" Being a troubleshooting engineer who likes solutions, I hypothesized that the entire Bible is about God giving us clues to find the "Tree of Life." We are to find it, then eat of its fruit and live forever. It is probably right under our noses, but we are so caught up in nega-tive, unimportant things of life, that we are not even looking for it. This hypothesis generated much enthusiasm and encouraged me to keep reading the Bible. I thought that finding the Tree of Life would be the greatest scientific and archeological find of all times. My steadfast motto became: "There is a Tree of Life, and I am going to find it!"

I believed in God, and I also believed the Bible to be true, but I could not understand why people were so easily fooled throughout the whole Bible. Adam and Eve were not too bright. Samson had great muscles, but nothing between his ears, or why would he have trusted Delilah again? (Judges 16) Delilah asked Samson what would take away his strength? Every time he told her something like, "If I were tied with seven cords I would lose my strength," the next morning would come and Samson would be tied with seven cords. This happened several times, and then he told Delilah, "If my hair is cut, my strength will depart." Delilah cut his hair and Samson's enemies poked his eyes out. How could Samson not figure out that he would be in danger?

I believed God could part the Red Sea, but how could the Egyptians be so stupid as to run in after the Israelites? The Israelites in the desert? After all the signs God sent them, they still complained against Him. Moses asked those Israelites who were with God to go to one side, and those against Him to go to the other. After the ground swallowed them up, I thought: "Dah! Couldn't you figure it out?" During the whole Bible, the Devil so easily tricked man into breaking each covenant with God. Then I would pray, "Oh God, the solution is so simple. You are creating these people too dumb. If you made them smarter, the world would not have so many problems." The mystery of God not making people smarter was baffling.

DAVID AND GOLIATH

My favorite Bible story is about a battle between the mountains. David and the people of Israel were on one mountain, and Goliath and the Philistines were on the other mountain. Every day for 40 days, Goliath, a nine-foot giant, would come out and say to the Israelites: "Your God is a joke, and you guys are wimps. Send your best man to fight me, one on one. If he wins, we will be your slaves. If I win, you will be our slaves." When the Israelites saw him coming they all hid in fear. No one would stand up to Goliath. However, David made what engineers call a breakthrough in technology.

I have a patent on heat exchangers, and the dream of every inventor is to come up with a breakthrough in technology that gives an advantage over all the competition and corners the market place. David is going to take his breakthrough in technology and make conventional weapons obsolete. You all know what happened. When David went out to meet Goliath, he stopped at a brook and pulled out five smooth stones. I thought: "Five stones? You are the inventor, David, you know you are going to get him in one shot, maybe two, but five?" Throughout the whole Bible, it seemed that in some parts, too many details were given, and in other parts, not enough. Anyway, David took the five smooth stones and put them into his shepherd's script. He rushed out with his sling and the first stone crushed Goliath's head. David cut Goliath's wounded head off and the people of God won. (1 Samuel 17)

CLUES FOR FINDING THE TREE OF LIFE

As I continued to struggle through the Bible, I was ready to give up on the theory of the "Tree of Life" until I read Proverbs 3:17: "Her ways are beautiful ways, all Her paths are peace. She is a Tree of Life to them that lay hold of Her, and he that retains Her is blessed." I thought, "Aha, a clue." I had no idea what the phrase meant, but at least the Bible mentioned it. At the end of the Bible, the Book of Revelations talks about a struggle. "He that has an ear, let him hear what the Spirit said to the churches: "To him that overcomes it, I will give to eat of the 'Tree of Life' which is in the paradise of my God." (Revelations 2:7) I thought, "Aha, a clue. There it is again." And the very last chapter of the entire Bible talks about the "Tree of Life." I knew it was important, and although I had an ear, I still did not understand it.

The New Testament was also a mystery. Often I wished I had been present to witness Jesus' miracles for myself. However, I did admire Jesus' zeal for always wanting to do the will of the Father. The problem was I did not know what exactly was the "will of the Father."

The Cross was a baffling contradiction. A progressive society is supposed to make life easier. Jesus' words, "Deny yourself, pick up your cross and come follow Me," seemed to make things harder. However, I could not deny that whenever I looked at the big Crucifix in the church where I grew up, my heart was touched, and it made me want to do good.

STILL DIDN'T UNDERSTAND

After finishing the Bible, I realized that I still did not know one thing about the Catholic faith. Not one! This was very frustrating. I could calculate Einstein's relativistic effect the earth's gravity had on light rays, but I could not tell you one thing that was going on in the Mass.

After struggling for so long, I was forced to come up with a frightening conclusion. They say the left side of the brain is for math and science, and the right side of the brain is for liberal arts. I was never very good at liberal arts. Religion must be so far right-brained that I was never going to understand anything. I had come to the conclusion that I was right-brain retarded, and that's just the way it was. Realizing that my method to analyze Medjugorje was all wrong, I changed from a religious to a scientific approach, something I could handle.

CHAPTER THREE -
FIRST TRIP TO MEDJUGORJE

The thought of going to Medjugorje stayed with me for six years, but a multiple of excuses postponed the trip. Then, an eight-year-old boy kept barging in on my memory repeating: "The Mother of God appeared for so long, and you did not go to see the miracles for yourself? How could you miss that opportunity?" That eight-year-old was myself. A number of years ago, my Grandma had told me about Our Lady appearing to the three shepherd children at Fatima, Portugal in 1917. I scolded her for not going. She explained that she was only twelve years old, and that her family was poor, and traveling then was not as easy as today. "Lame excuses, you could have found a way on a boat had you really tried."

The memory of that scolding haunted me. "What excuse am I going to give my grandchildren for not exploring Medjugorje?"

In December of 1989, I signed up with a group that went to Medjugorje. The "Tree of Life" had to be somewhere in that part of the world, and traveling there might help provide the missing clues.

While on the plane, fellow pilgrims were telling me how they had seen the sun dancing and spinning. I believed they were telling the truth; however, these simple people from this backward country would not know a high-tech laser show when they saw one. My plan was to map out where the electricity was running and pick out possible laser projection sites. When everyone was looking at the miracle of the sun, I would go to the projection site and say, "Gotcha," pat myself on the back, and say, "All in a weeks work."

On arriving in Medjugorje, one lady started to poke me on the shoulder and say, "Guy, don't you feel that great peace?" "How do you feel peace?" I thought.

"Medjugorje is such a small town, so proving the laser show theory is going to be easier than I expected. This is going to be like shooting fish in a barrel. This town has only one road," I chuckled. Saint James Church had two large bell towers. There were some homes and souvenir shops. Cross Mountain or Mount Krizevac; a steep mountain speckled with rocks, green trees, and bushes was on one end, and across the field of grapes was Mount Podbrdo. Mount Podbrdo had even more rocks, but was smaller than Mount Krizevac. Mount Podbrdo is also known as Apparition Hill because Our Lady first appeared to the children here. According to the visionaries, this is also the location where a lasting miraculous sign will be left until the end of time to prove the authenticity of Our Lady's appearance.

During the first few days, I did not witness anything unusual. Reading some of Our Lady's messages convinced half of me to believe in their truth, but I was still pretty confused. It seemed that the whole week was going to pass with no miracles, and I felt gypped.

Wanting to force the issue, I climbed on top of Mount Krizevac and said a prayer to Our Lady. I had never prayed to Our Lady before. Nothing in Roman Catholicism made sense to me, and Marian devotion seemed silly. "I pray directly to God myself. What do I need Her for? And that Rosary, that silly prayer for little old ladies. What about us engineers? We need prayers too." So I challenged Our Lady with my ideas. The visionaries described the Virgin Mary as an 18-year-old Girl, so I talked to Her as I would talk to any 18-year-old girl. Standing by the 14-ton cross, I said, "Hey, Mary, it's me, Guy. I come here from Chicago. I'll tell You what, give me Your best shot, and I'm going to give You my best shot. If You win, I will do whatever You say. If I win, I'm going to defeat Medjugorje."

My first unusual experience took place when I lifted up the Rosary and attempted to say, "What is it with this silly weapon?" Something prevented me from saying it, and I could not even say it internally from the heart. I thought, "This is strange, THERE MUST BE SOME LOGICAL EXPLANATION FOR THIS!!! I am acting silly, and somehow my subconscious must be taking over and suppressing me from acting more silly and saying these things out loud." Instead of talking, I held the Rosary in the air in a gesture that expressed my thoughts: "You are kidding about wanting me to pray this, aren't You?" I felt in my heart that the challenge was happily accepted. Zipping down the mountain, I eagerly awaited and prepared for the coming miracle.

On December 8th, the feast of the Immaculate Conception, our group came out of Mass. It was one o'clock in the afternoon, and about 50 people started to see the miracle of the sun. They claimed to see the sun dance, spin, and display colors and sacred images. When I looked up, it burned my eyes. "THERE MUST BE SOME LOGICAL EXPLANA-

TION FOR THIS. It is a high-tech laser show and I am at a bad angle. You have to be over by them to see it." I was looking for underground wires at the time and was separated from the group. On joining the others, I looked up, and the sun burned my eyes again. Putting on sunglasses and looking at the sun while directly behind someone's head resulted in me getting my eyes burned again.

This was baffling and had me pacing back and forth. I was thinking, "Physics taught that there is nothing anyone could do to stop the solar radiation from burning the retina. Therefore, I must be the only idiot who is looking at the sun, and everyone else must be squinting." While recording their observations with a tape recorder and walking around to the front side of the people, I found their eyes wide open. Now logic dictated that I should be able to see it also. Looking up only caused my eyes to get burned again. Now I got stuck in trying to find a logical explanation and I looked at eight peoples' open eyes and my eyes got burned each time, and finally the pain was so severe, I had to leave.

Pain seized my head, my mind was filled with confusion, and black spots covered my eyes as I stumbled down the road from St. James Church to Mount Krizevac. When I tried to figure out what had happened, I found myself repeating my name and address over and over. "This does not make sense, they should be blind for looking into the sun that long. I should be blind for looking into the sun that long." As I tripped into potholes and bounced off signs, fear and reality set in, and I thought, "Great, I'm blind." My parents and several of my friends had told me not to go to Medjugorje, and now I was going to return home and say, "Hi, I'm blind!" I was so angry because if anyone should have known better, it should have been me. In anger, I started kicking myself all around Medjugorje.

The image of me being blind and my friends laughing at me

was pure torture. Throughout the years, I had made fun of many people for doing stupid things. Thinking of them, I realized that I was more stupid than any of them. Thinking of the Bible, in a few moments, I thought of excuses for everyone except myself. Even the Egyptians faced certain death for disobeying Pharaoh, so it was logical for them to take their chances by going into the Red Sea. The thought of doing the most stupid thing in the history of the human race had me completely humiliated.

It seemed like even the rocks in Medjugorje were laughing at me. As I took the turn from Mount Krizevac over to Mount Podbrdo, the fear and realization of being blind for the rest of my life started to overwhelm me, and I began to grovel very humbly, begging God, "I will do whatever You say for the rest of my life. Please give me my sight back." After stumbling up Apparition Hill, I sat down on a rock, as part of me was trying to figure out what had happened, and the other part was groveling and making several promises to God on what I would do if I received my sight back.

I did not see Her or hear Her, but something strange started going on in my heart. It was as if Our Lady were brushing me off, (I was full of dirt), and saying, "Jesus forgives, Jesus forgives, Jesus forgives, Jesus forgives, Jesus forgives," and then She said, "Do you want to help?" "Sure!" I replied. With that, She kissed me on the forehead.

Now, if you look at the sun, your eyes not only hurt, but you will get a terrible pain above the bridge of your nose. This pain was so unbearable; it felt like someone took a baseball bat and whacked my forehead. When Our Lady gave me this kiss, my forehead was filled with a warm tingling sensation, the piercing pain left me, my eyes cleared up, and I was happy because I could see again. Actually, I ran down Apparition Hill and across the fields shouting, "Yes! Yes! Yes!" and went home.

4

CHAPTER FOUR -
LIFE WITH THE WEAPON

Upon returning home, I sent letters to my friends describing the Medjugorje events. Figuring, "These guys are no dummies, they can figure it out for themselves." I also realized that I had to live Our Lady's messages. Even though I had no doubt that Medjugorje was true, the problem was I still thought the Rosary was a little old lady's prayer. Prayer itself was very difficult for me. It took time, I was easily distracted, and I did not see the point in prayer. Taking a calculator, I said to Our Lady, "Three Rosaries a day is saying one thousand seventy one Hail Mary's a week! That is too much. I think Sunday Mass and one Our Father, one Hail Mary, and one Glory Be a week is enough. What do you think about those apples?" Remembering that Our Lady won fair and square in Medjugorje, I compromised and prayed five decades of the Rosary each day.

The first two things I understood about the faith became clear upon returning home from Medjugorje.

One: You don't go up to the top of Mount Krizevac and give the Mother of God any grief.

Two: Something Vicka, one of the visionaries in Medjugorje, said, "Even though we don't think so, Jesus and Mary are always very close to you, but you have to open up your hearts, so you will realize by your heart how much They love you." It was like looking through a two-way mirror. This closeness was now obvious.

Even with these two pieces of knowledge about the faith, I still did not like praying the Rosary. So I would be praying the Rosary and after a short while I would say, "Hail Mary, full of grace, this is an insult to my intelligence..., Hail Mary full of grace, this is an insult to my intelligence...," And as I would pray this way, I would relive that experience in Medjugorje. I could feel the sun burning my eyes that made a sharp pain in my forehead, and I would get totally humiliated and scared and start shaking and then say, "O.k., O.k. I'm praying, I'm praying." This did not go on for only one or two days, this went on every day for about three months.

At the end of three months, I would pray the Rosary, and soon my attitude would altar the prayer to "Hail Mary full of grace, this is an insult to my intelligence," and then I would experience the feeling of the sun burning my eyes and start shaking. One time, I yelled out in anger to the corner of the room, where I imagined Our Lady was floating: "Stop that, I can't help it if this is a dumb prayer!" Then I slapped the Rosary pamphlet on the table and said, "Look at this, it does not even make sense. The fruit of the mystery for the First Joyful Mystery, The Annunciation, is humility. What does humility have to do with the Annunciation? I don't get it. Humility is what you did to me in Medjugorje. You bopped me on the head, just like David bopped Goliath on the head!" And then, the light went on. "I get it!" I remembered the kids from Medjugorje and Padre Pio calling the Rosary "the weapon." Many things in the Old Testemant foreshadow the fullfilment in the New Testemant. Holding the crucifix of the Rosary in my hand made it resemble a sling. *"David's sling just prefigured the true weapon, which is the Rosary. And the five smooth stones David pulled out of the brook represented the five decades of the Rosary."* Swinging the Rosary around helped analyze the puzzle. "David struck Goliath with the first stone, and the fruit of the first mystery is humility. God is going to use the humility of the Blessed Mother to crush the proud head of Satan." After figuring this out, I sprang to my feet and started to pat myself on the back. "Now I know three things about the faith." Then I stopped, and thought, "Wait a minute, I am on the wrong side, and I am on the receiving end of this weapon."

I use to think that when I died, I would go straight to Heaven. Many times since my conversion, I have found myself on the wrong side. In Medjugorje, I went to Confession for the first time in ten years. My soul was in the state of mortal sin. After my conversion, I paid more attention to the faith. The faith would touch on areas regarding mortal sin. It seemed that everytime I learned something new, I found out I was on the road to Hell. However, Our Lady is good, and She will work with you.

Our Lady had promised in Medjugorje: "Pray, and one day prayer will become a joy for you." Prayer was such a struggle for me that I longed for the day it would become a joy. Since prayer is an exercise, it was like taking up jogging and experiencing cramps. Only after proper conditioning would the cramps go away and jogging becomes easier. It took a long time, but I have come to realize that the Rosary is a powerful weapon and a thinking prayer, which is an expression of love. With grace and patience from Our Lady, I have come to enjoy the fifteen/twenty decades of the Rosary every day. Our Lady says, "The Rosary is the Solution."

CHAPTER FIVE - DAILY BATTLE

I not only struggled with the Rosary, but also with all of Her messages. I viewed Mary as an eighteen-year-old girl with a peace plan that comprised of conversion, praying the Rosary, fasting, Confession, the Holy Mass, and reading the Bible. Because She won fair and square, I felt obliged to do what She asked for, no matter how silly it seemed to me.

Many times I have wondered what Our Lady meant up on Apparition Hill by the phrase, "Do you want to help?" When it came to religion, I knew nothing, felt nothing, and understood nothing. I was a complete "spiritual dud" with no talent in religion whatsoever. I could not sing, talk eloquently to groups, or write, and I did not even like fussing with things related to religion. "Shouldn't you be bugging a philosophy or psychology major for help? What could a chemical process engineer possibly do for you?" "Do you need a new process or a plan for something?" After a while, I thought that She might need help with Her peace plan. Our Lady's peace plan seemed ridiculous. "This is no solution to obtain peace," I thought. "People are rational creatures, they need a plan that is complete with logic and science. If you want to convert them, you have to show them all the scientific test work that was done in Medjugorje, by the University of Milan, and the medical facility of Mount Pelier. When people see the data for themselves, they will listen and respond. What is prayer and fasting going to do? Prayer is boring. You are going to bore them to death. Fasting? You are going to starve them to death. Confession? You are going to scare them to death. I get it, when they die, You will say, 'rest in peace.'" As I would start laughing at Our Lady and Her plan, I would relive that experience in Medjugorje, where the sun blinded my eyes, and I felt completely humiliated. Soon, I found myself saying, "Cut that out! I can't help it if it is a dumb plan. Am I not entitled to my opinion? Is this not America? Just because all Your faithful dodo birds do whatever You tell them without thinking, I think for myself. I know a dumb plan when I see one. That is my job You know. Look! We can resolve this in a scientific way. For a test, we will use two people. On one person, we will try to use my way to convert them. For the other person, Your way. You will see."

After selecting two people for the test, I made a lame effort to observe Her way for the first participant, and I worked very hard on a presentation of the facts for the second. They were both typical Church-on-Sunday Catholics. To my surprise, the first person had an impressive conversion.

To the second person, I explained how experts in psychology, psychotherapy, medicine, and spiritual theology testify that the visionaries are perfectly normal and balanced. They were able to rule out every possible explanation that the origin of the visions were in natural causes. Then, I showed him the actual charts and data collected by the scientists who tested the visionaries using tools including electro-encephalogram (for brain activity), electrocardiogram (heart activity), and electro-oculogram (eye activity). The specialists from the prestigious Milan and Montpelier Universities in France said the apparitions were scientifically inexplicable.

To my frustration, the second person rejected everything in a very illogical fashion. I became angry, so I attempted to exercise conversion by force. My persistence and some insults, over time, only made the situation worse. Actually, I became afraid that this person was going to leave the Church entirely. This fear found me completely abandoning my mode of evangelization and begging Our Lady for help because I did not want to be responsible for the discouragement of a soul.

It would have been so much easier and made so much more sense had I only found the "Tree of Life." Then I would just eat the fruit of it and live forever. However, the struggle continued. I tried for a whole year to convince Our Lady that Her plan had flaws, and it took that whole year for me to start to realize the truth and power behind living Her messages. Several times, after realizing that I had been acting like a complete blockhead, I asked Her why She didn't ask God to zap me out of existence for my attitude. Her patience is truly amazing.

Also, during that year, I sent several letters to my engineering friends. Oftentimes, I would tell Our Lady, "I'm worried about these guys. Look at what a tough time I am having with Your messages, and I believe they are true. What is going to happen to them?"

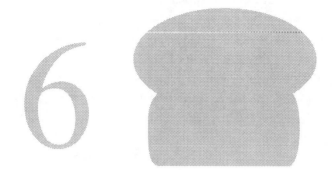

CHAPTER SIX - FASTING

The daily battle with Our Lady intensified with Her message of fasting. In my mind, the thought of fasting was strongly associated with doing physical damage to one's body. "The good God gave us a body. Instead of using our brains to take care of it, are we suppose to starve it?"

The message Our Lady gave was clear: to fast on bread and water on Wednesdays and Fridays. This was so unreasonable and radical that I decided to compromise and fast a half-day on Wednesday, and if it did not kill me, maybe in the future I would try more. Wednesday was chosen because "Friday night" was already designated for poker, beer, and pizza with the guys.

After skipping breakfast for the first time, light-headedness and dizziness set in. This did cause me to think of all the hungry and needy people in the world; I would eat supper in the evening, but their hunger would continue. When lunchtime passed, it seemed the feeling of death was approaching, and my body hit the floor. Listening to the Medjugorje tape recordings had me hoping that there might be some way around the fasting part.

The visionary named Vicka stated, "If you are fasting and have headaches or feel dizzy, with strong faith in Jesus and the Blessed Mother, such things would not be appearing."

"What! I have plenty of faith, it just happens to be bad advice, that's all. Fasting is bad science." As I lay "dying" on the floor (to prove my point), I started to read a book on fasting. To my surprise, the book showed that from a scientific standpoint, a 24-hour fast on bread and water is healthy for your body. Instantaneously recovering, I sprung to my feet, "What! Fasting is good for you?" Fasting actually cleanses your liver of all the toxins that build up from the food we eat. I have often wondered how many cancer cases that are attributed to the preservatives, additives, and pollutants that our bodies are exposed to.

It took me several months to work up to the full two days of fasting. It was particularly difficult to wait until midnight on Friday, when friends were enjoying pizza.

Besides making us physically healthy, fasting has a twofold benefit:

1. In a moral sense, fasting is a great spiritual exercise in mortification that helps one gain control over the physical senses. We must fight the good fight. (2Timothy 4:7) It is important to rule over the body and not have the body rule over us.

2. From a spiritual sense, prayer and fasting can cast out demons. (Matthew 17:20) Our Lady makes it very clear that much of the trouble in the world today comes from losing spiritual battles.

Fast out of love for God and in gratitude for all He gives you.

Additional advice on fasting includes:

1. Understand the importance of fasting and offer it up as a sacrifice to God.

2. Do what you can for starters, even half a day.

3. Beg God for the grace to fast.

4. Drink lots of water, as Our Lady advises.

5. Increase fasting time, as you are able.

6. Thank God as you get the grace to fast.

7. Eat healthy and nutritious foods on the non-fast days, especially green vegetables as Daniel, the prophet, did.

CHAPTER SEVEN - CONFESSION

Our Lady asked for monthly Confession. If you need proof of the reality of spiritual battles between good and evil, experience the illogical, childish fears one encounters before going to the Sacrament of Confession after an extended period of time. I thought it was safe to go to Confession halfway around the world in the little town of Medjugorje. Upon leaving the confessional, I felt as if boulders had been removed from my heart. This feeling caught me by surprise because I did not think I had boulders on my heart to begin with. What a deal! If a soul overcomes fear, is obedient to the precepts of the Church, and goes to Confession, then Jesus Christ will personally touch that soul with His Grace and Mercy, strengthen it, and give it a fresh start to life. If not, the soul takes all his sins to the Throne of God on Judgment Day. Our Lady has told us that we must experience Jesus' healing power in the Sacrament of Mercy.

Our Lady appeared at Fatima, Portugal in 1917. Our Lady's promise at Fatima about practicing the Five First Saturdays, which includes Confession, encouraged me to go to Confession once a month for five months in a row. Every month I was afraid, and it was easy for me to imagine myself kicking and screaming as Our

Lady dragged me into Confession. After completing the Five First Saturdays, these childish fears left me, and Confession became easy to continue after that. At Fatima, Our Lady pronounced one powerful promise that would come with this devotion that God would send Her at the hour of our death with enough graces for salvation. After walking around with my soul in a state of mortal sin for so many years, this promise was comforting. Besides, who wants to go to Hell? There is no future in it.

CHAPTER EIGHT -
THE EUCHARIST AND DAILY MASS

Over a year after going to Medjugorje and struggling with all Our Lady's messages, I listened to the audiotape I recorded on that first trip. In one of her talks, Vicka said, "The most important and holiest of all the moments is during the Holy Mass. At that moment, Jesus comes alive, and we are to receive Him in our hearts."

"What?" I exclaimed. Even though I grew up with a Catholic education, it seemed that I had never heard this before. Looking at the corner where I imagined Our Lady floating, I said, "Are you trying to tell me that the Eucharist we are receiving at Mass is not bread, but God under the appearance of bread? I work on complicated flow sheets. I have to keep track of all the energy involved and make the best use out of all the BTU's (energy). Are you trying to tell me that something more powerful than a firecracker, more powerful than a stick of dynamite, more powerful than a nuclear bomb, or even the sun, more powerful than all the galaxies in the universe combined–that God Himself has been going into my mouth every Sunday for all these years, and I had no clue whatsoever? NO WAY! I'M NOT THAT STUPID!" I then picked up a pillow and started to throw it at Her. As I focused in on my target in the corner of the room, I realized that no one was there. Asking myself, "Who am I throwing this pillow at? Who am I arguing with all the time? How come I have to lose every argument? I am not going to lose this one!" So I stormed out of the room and went to the Library (University of Chicago) to do research. "Look, when You bopped me on the head in Medjugorje, it was pretty stupid of me to look at the sun, but You caught me off guard. However, there is no way something as powerful as God could have been going into my mouth my whole life without me being aware of it. There is no way I could have missed that."

After I arrived at the library, I looked through several books. I found *The Ancient Christian Writers*, by James A. Kleist, S.J. to be very helpful. The teachings of the early Church fathers were unanimous: the Eucharist is God, the Eucharist is God, the number one truth of our faith, the Eucharist is God. They reference several Bible passages to support this, including, the Last Supper accounts in the Gospels of Matthew (26), Mark (14), and Luke (22), when Jesus utters the words of institution: "This is My Body" and "This is My Blood," and the detailed description of the Eucharist in the sixth chapter of John. Jesus said, "I am the living bread, which came down from Heaven. If any man shall eat this bread, he shall live forever. And the bread that I give is My flesh for the life of the world... He that eats my flesh and drinks My blood has everlasting life, and I will raise him up on the last day... Unless you eat of the flesh of the Son of Man, and drink His blood, you have no life within you... He that eats My flesh and drinks My blood will live in Me and I in him." (John 6:51-2, 55-7)

"It is true!" I thought, "Our Lady is right again." I challenge any engineer to research this for yourself, and I guarantee that after a few hours, you will be convinced this is what Jesus meant, and the early Christians understood it that way also. The Church holds fast to this truth even today. (*New Catechism of the Catholic Church* #1323)

Understanding this with your head is easy, but it can be very difficult to believe it in your heart. On the way home, I stopped at a Perpetual Adoration Chapel, where Jesus in the Eucharist is adored 24 hours a day. I knelt down before the Host in the beautiful gold monstrance with my new found knowledge, but my heart said, "I don't get it. I see bread there, I don't see God." Upon further contemplation, the words from Scripture overwhelmed me. "This is the will of My Father... that every one who looks at the Son, and believes in Him may have life everlasting." (John 6:40) With that realization, I became very fearful, because I knew exactly what that meant. I had to look at the Host (Son) and believe that It was Jesus, but I didn't believe it. "Oh no, I'm going to hell again," I thought. I stood up to run out of the chapel, but something strange started going on in my heart. It was Our Lady grabbing me by the hand and saying, "Don't think you know everything! Pray that God will give you the grace to understand." In my heart, I grabbed onto Her hand and said, "Look, Our Lady, You are not going anywhere. You are staying with me. You got me in this, now You have to stay with me to help!" Kneeling down, I prayed, "Dear God, I'm sorry I slept in your Church and did not pay attention for so many years. Please give me the grace to understand."

My heart understood that it was going to take time, so I started making weekly visits to the Perpetual Adoration Chapel. What baffled me was at first, I believed Our Lady was there, next to Her Son in adoration, but I did not believe yet, that Jesus was there. With time, grace, prayer, and study, my faith started to increase.

This experience marked a turning point in my relationship with Our Lady. Before this, Her presence was nice, but afterwards, I embraced Her as a child embracing his mother.

Over time, I also came to realize that the Holy Mass is the greatest form of worship to God. Receiving Jesus by means of the Holy Eucharist became the highlight of my day. "I gotta have Jesus!"

CHAPTER NINE -
SECOND TRIP TO MEDJUGORJE

In April 1991, I took my second trip to Medjugorje. This time, an engineering friend, whom I will call Gerald, also went. It felt great to be back in Medjugorje. Something about Medjugorje touches your soul and makes you feel at home. The Blessed Mother appeared every day to the visionaries and blessed the people. A few days into the trip, during the time the visionaries had the visit from the Blessed Mother, Gerald and I saw the miracle of the sun. The miracle resembled a total eclipse of the sun with a white Host, Holy Communion, that replaced the black moon and blocked the sun's rays from burning our eyes. Both of us looked away and noted that we did not have the black spots in our eyes that are caused by looking at a bright light. In my heart, I was very thankful to our Lady because She urged me to beg God for the grace to understand His presence in Holy Communion. I had been growing in faith, and this miraculous sign helped.

Later on that evening, I read a book, while Gerald paced the floor, back and forth, trying to digest the events that day. He said, "Guy, I don't think we saw a miracle today."

"Oh yeah?" I replied and continued to read the book. After pacing some more he said, "We don't try to look at the sun at home. It was

6:40 in the evening and the sun was low enough in the sky that our eyes happened to adjust to it enough to make it look like there was a white disc in the sun."

"Oh yeah!" I replied and continued to read the book. Then he mumbled that he would have to see it again at the same time of day and have it burn his eyes before he would believe. "What did you say?" I asked with great joy. With a loud voice he said, "I would have to see it at the same time of day and have it burn my eyes before I will believe!"

"You heard him Blessed Mother," I thought while imagining a bull's eye being drawn on Gerald's forehead.

The next day we were in church at the time of the apparition and Gerald said, "Come on, Guy, let's go see the miracle."

"That's okay, Gerald, I'm staying here and praying." So I stayed for the Rosary and Mass, and came outside afterwards only to find Gerald sitting on a bench with his hand covering his eyes. After I said "hello," he remarked without taking his hand off of his eyes, "Okay, I believe it now."

Later on Gerald described how others saw the miracle, and this time it had burned his eyes.

CHAPTER TEN -
FINDING THE TREE OF LIFE

After returning home to the USA, I had renewed confidence that Our Lady had a definite "in" with God. My personal communication with Our Lady consisted of reading Her messages and when a certain situation arose, a light would go on, and I would know which message applied. It is similar to taking a test in school. You study, you are asked a question, your mind goes blank, then the light goes on, and you know the answer. My return from Medjugorje helped this; it was very easy to imagine the Blessed Virgin Mary floating around the room the same way the visionaries saw Her.

I asked Our Lady in prayer: "Ok, Blessed Mother, what about the 'Tree of Life?' Where do I find it?" In my heart I understood, "Pray the Rosary for all you ask of Me." Not happy with this answer, I reluctantly started praying the Rosary.

The First Joyful Mystery went well. In the next mystery, Mary, with God inside of Her, visits Her cousin, Elizabeth to help her during her pregnancy. I tried to meditate. I imagined that Our Lady was riding on a donkey through the hill country. I started to look at the trees. During my prayer, I started daydreaming about the "Tree of Life." "If I could only find the 'Tree of Life,' everything else would make more sense. What clue did I miss? What kind of fruit grows on it? Maybe apples or cherries? Whatever it is, it must be a very special fruit." With that thought, the Mystery of the Rosary came back to me. Mary was standing in front of Her cousin. Elizabeth was filled with the Holy Spirit when she saw Mary. She cried out in a loud voice: "Blessed are you among women and BLESSED IS THE FRUIT OF THY WOMB."

"FRUIT!" I gasped. "FRUIT OF THY WOMB! BLESSED MOTHER, IT IS YOU! You are the true 'Tree of Life,' and the fruit that we are to eat and live forever is the fruit of Your womb, Jesus, particularly the Eucharist, which is Jesus under the appearance of bread. At last, I have found You! I want to live forever!" The living God wants to live inside of us also. I just stood there with my mouth open for a long time, looking at the corner of the room where I imagined the Blessed Mother was floating and studied this mystery from God.

CHAPTER ELEVEN -
CONSECRATION TO JESUS THROUGH MARY

In the summer of 1991, numerous prayer groups started on ac-
count of the reported apparitions of the Blessed Virgin Mary to
Joseph Reinholtz at the Queen of Heaven Cemetery in Hillside,
Illinois. I began "pilgrimaging" around Chicago-land to more
and more prayer groups. In late summer of that year, my grand-
mother asked me to take her shopping. I replied, "Sorry Gram,
I am going to a prayer group," to which she shouted, "You're
falling in love with the Blessed Virgin Mary!"

"What? That is sick!" I blasted her. Good–ol Grandma, God rest
her soul, stared me down with her big blue eyes and said it again
even louder. "You are falling in love with the Blessed Mother."
I made a gesture that I was not going to argue with someone who
is obviously wrong, and I walked out of the room.

My face was turning red, and I started thinking, "You know, I
have been acting pretty strangely this last year and a half: fasting,
going to prayer groups, daily Mass, conferences, pilgrimages, and
reading everything about Mary. Am I in love with the Blessed
Mother?" Something seemed so strange about this concept of

love for the Blessed Mother. "Oh no, I am going to Hell again!"

Months back, a little old lady from a prayer group gave me a book written by Saint Louis DeMontfort entitled *True Devotion*. It discussed something about being a holy slave of love to Our Blessed Mother, so I threw it in the "to be read maybe someday" pile. With my face flushed red, I now frantically looked for the book. When I found it, I began reading and to my surprise, St. Louis DeMontefort claimed, "Holy slavery of love to the Blessed Virgin Mary is a good thing." Actually, he wrote that it is the easiest, surest, and fastest way to obtain union with God and thus become a saint. The key is to embrace the kingdom of Heaven as a child, (Matthew 18:17) and to imitate Jesus, the perfect Child, Who honored His father and mother and was subject to them. (Luke 2:51) Saint Louis DeMontfort gives us an example. He describes two men who presented gifts to their king. The proud man gives the apple directly to the king. Because it had a worm in it, the king was offended and had the man beheaded. The humble man gave an apple to the queen to present to the king. The good queen cut out the worms, put it on a silver platter, and added the king's favorite spices to it. The king was so impressed with the gift that he considered the man part of his family. Because pride once caused so much trouble in Heaven, God is very pleased with "True Devotion." "I'm not going to Hell?" I thought. "I'm going to like this devotion, since I already promised our Lady after that episode in Medjugorje that I would do everything She says. If I love Her in a holy way, it is a good thing."

I was impatient to wait over two months to start the 33 day preparation for consecration on a recommended day, so I completed it on October 4, 1991, the feast of Saint Francis of Assisi.

To my pleasant surprise, St. Louis DeMontfort writes in his preparation for Total Consecration, that Mary is the true Tree of Life. (*True Devotion* Numbers 213-225)

I found out first hand that practicing St. Louis DeMontfort's devotion is very powerful and that it could change anyone's life.

NOTE: During our fall 1998 pilgrimage to Medjugorje, a physician accompanied us. He was very impressed with Medjugorje and said it was changing his life. I asked him to proofread this paper and upon completing his review, he asked, "Is Mary like a God?"

"Next to God, Mary is less than an atom," I replied. "However, people have a hard time with the truth: 'He that is mighty has done great things for Her,' (Luke 1:49), because we do not appreciate the great things God is going to do for us as His adopted children. Remember, 'Eye has not seen, ear has not heard...' which means, we cannot even imagine our great reward. How much greater of a reward does She deserve?"

During our conversation, I could tell he was still struggling with the concept. He said, "In church they crowned Her statue and sang songs to Her." His four year–old daughter came up to him and said, "Goodnight Daddy," and gave him a hug and a kiss. I asked him, "Was that display of affection offensive to God? You are God's gift to her and He provides for her through you. It is the same way with Mother Mary. She is God's gift to us. God provides good things for us through Her." I could tell by the expression on his face that he understood.

On the way home, I heard the song "Little Drummer Boy" playing on the radio. I remembered my struggles to understand Baby Jesus. I thought of my little efforts to please Jesus and Mary and a tear rolled down the side of my cheek.

CHAPTER TWELVE - HIGHLIGHTS

During the exciting times we live in, we see more problems, chaos, and wake-up calls. Several people offer solutions from a purely human way of thinking that only make matters worse. To obtain a true solution for our world's ills, keep in mind seven thoughts: God's Plan, Five First Saturdays, Divine Mercy, Consecration to Jesus through Mary, Medjugorje, Eucharistic Covenant, and Love Jesus.

1. GOD'S PLAN

The plan for our world is to read and live Our Lady's messages. God sent Her. Conversion, pray the Rosary (the weapon) with your heart, go to Confession, attend Holy Mass (receive fruit from the "Tree of Life" to live forever), read the Bible, fast, and peace. This is vital, and it makes sense once one realizes that there is a spiritual battle going on. (Revelations 12, Ephesians 6:11-12) Living these messages is your greatest school. You will learn more about a life of grace through this struggle to overcome the world and yourself, than any book or university can teach you. If you want a place to start, Our Lady recommends praying the Peace Rosary every day: The Apostles Creed, seven Our Fathers, seven Hail Marys, and seven Glory Be's.

This "Plan" is not only for us in these "Last Days," during which God will use Our Lady to crush Satan's head, but it is also for the people after "these times." Our Lady's messages are not only the best way to fight Satan, but they are also the best way to love Jesus and to provide the tools necessary to help others love Jesus. This is what evangelization is all about. The one who loves Jesus is teaching us how to love Jesus.

2. FATIMA–FIVE FIRST SATURDAYS

To help with conversions, practice and promote the Fatima Five First Saturday devotion. Our Lady's request from the apparitions at Fatima, Portugal starting on May 13, 1917, is an extremely important tool for obtaining Grace and Mercy for our world today. Our Lady asked the faithful, for five consecutive first Saturdays of the month to:

I. Pray five decades of the Rosary.

II. Go to Mass and receive Communion.

III. Go to Confession (within eight days before or
      after first Saturday.)

IV. Meditate for 15 minutes on the 15/20 mysteries of
      the Rosary.

V. Offer all this up in reparation for the sins and blasphemies
      against the Immaculate Heart of Mary.

The promises of this devotion include that no matter what else happens in your life, God will grant enough graces so that you will not suffer the eternal fires of Hell.

In 1917, Our Lady asked for the consecration of Russia. She said that Russia would become a super power, and annihilate many nations, and persecute the Church. This prediction seemed silly because Russia was not so impressive as a country. In May 1905, the Japanese Navy virtually annihilated a large Russian fleet in the decisive battle of Tsushima. In 1917, Russia was even struggling to feed their people. Nevertheless, history has proved how accurate this prophecy was. To STOP THIS from happening, Our Lady asked the faithful to practice the Five First Saturday devotion, and for the Holy Father in union with all the bishops in the world to consecrate Russia to the Immaculate Heart of Mary. Before 1984, this had not been done.

Pope John Paul II was shot on May 13, 1981, the Fatima anniversary. The bullet miraculously was deflected as it traveled through his body, preventing it from striking any vital organs. As he recovered, he called for the Fatima papers of 1917. After reading the papers and the future secrets, he traveled to Fatima and put the bullet in the crown of the statue of Our Lady, and said it was Her intercession that had spared his life.

Pope John Paul II consecrated the world to the Immaculate Heart of Mary on March 25, 1984. Our Lady reminds us in modern day apparitions that seeing Communism collapse, shortly after this, should give us renewed enthusiasm to practice Her request.

She also reminds us that we are overcome by our problems because they are humanly impossible to solve. It is very simple for God to solve them, so He, in all His wisdom and love for us, gives us this simple solution. In God's wisdom, He gives His children an opportunity to help. So practice and spread the Fatima Five First Saturdays. Our Lady says it is so important, and it will give meaning to your life.

Our Lady wants the Five First Saturdays to be practiced in every parish in the United States.

3. DIVINE MERCY

These are the times of God's great mercy. In Moses' day, God displayed to the world "His Great Power." With His only begotten Son Jesus, God displayed to the world "His Great Love." In these "Last Days," God will display to the world "His Great Mercy." Do not despair over the humiliating and miserable state of slavery in which sin has lead us. Call on God's infinite Mercy. Especially at three o'clock in the afternoon, the hour during which Jesus died. Pray the Chaplet of Divine Mercy as given to Saint Maria Faustina. Practice the A, B, C's of mercy: Ask for His Mercy; Be merciful; Complete trust.

Call Marian Helpers, 1-800-462-7426 and ask for pamphlet "MPL" to obtain more information.

4. CONSECRATION TO JESUS THROUGH MARY

If you need enthusiasm to do these things, then do the 33-day preparation for consecration by Saint Louis DeMontfort. (To obtain, *Preparation for Total Consecration*, write to the Montfort Fathers, Bayshore, New York 11706-8993, 631-665-0726.) If you want God to work powerfully in your life, try this true devotion. Pope John Paul II's motto was "Totus Tuus" or "Totally Yours." In Pope John Paul II's book, *Crossing the Threshold of Hope*, he describes working in a soda factory and thinking to give up his devotion to Mary and focus more on Jesus. At that time, he stumbled upon *True Devotion* by St. Louis DeMontfort, and found that practicing "True Devotion" was very "Christocentric." Look at the short time between his working in the soda factory and becoming Pope. It is phenomenal.

Mother Teresa of Calcutta has the fastest growing order of Sisters in the history of the Church. She recommends to all her novices to practice Saint Louis DeMontfort's Consecration and to spend one hour a day in Eucharistic adoration.

It doesn't matter how big a sinner you are. Note that in his writings St. Louis DeMontfort says that great saints would pop up in the "Last Days" (who practiced this devotion).

5. MEDJUGORJE

If you are in a rut and are unable do anything religious, go on a pilgrimage, especially to Medjugorje. (see www.medj1.com) Just try a little–God and Our Lady will do the rest. If you cannot travel, read a book or watch a video on Medjugorje and beg Our Lady for Her intercession with God. The Lord is pouring out powerful graces in Medjugorje, through Mary. Endeavor to obtain grace for your soul, so it might grow at peace with God. Conversion takes time. Do not wait to be converted! If it rains in the desert, flash floods cause damage. Choose to allow God to put life back into your soul. Then you can be that "Good Soil" upon which He can shower His graces abundantly.

Remember the parable that tells of Jesus' coming? The five wise virgins had extra oil for their lamps, but the five foolish ones ran out. If you are in a rut, chances are your light is going out. Go to Medjugorje and ask Our Lady to fill your lamp with oil. She will. Medjugorje is a special gift from God, who is providing conversions all over the world. Look at the alternative. We all know what happened to those with the empty lamps of oil.

6. THE EUCHARISTIC COVENANT

With all your heart: study, receive, and spend time with Jesus in the Eucharist. (John 6:26-72) Polls show that I am not the only one who did not know our Mighty God is coming into their mouth on Sunday. Only 20% of the Catholic people under the age of 50 have a clue. The Eucharist is not only the Fruit from the Tree of Life that we are to eat and live forever, but also the Covenant between God and His people. (Matthew 26:26-28) The Bible refers to the "Chosen Ones" as the ones who have the Covenant with God. Remember that the Jewish religion was temporary. It was to bridge the gap between Moses and the Christ. Jesus, the Son of God, personally instructed the disciples. Jesus Christ established the New and Everlasting Covenant with His "Chosen Ones" on Holy Thursday when He instituted the Eucharist.

In the Garden of Eden, the Devil could have tricked Adam and Eve in many ways, but he went after the Covenant with God. Just as he tried to get them to break the Covenant by eating the forbidden fruit so they would surely die; he endeavors to get us to break our Covenant by taking away the fruit from the Tree of Life that allows us to live forever. Profound ignorance regarding the Eucharist is no accident. The Devil's first step to take the Eucharist away from us is to cause this "smoke" of ignorance. Get yourself a copy of the *New Catechism of the Catholic Church* and read up on the Eucharist. Find a Perpetual Adoration Chapel, and for at least one hour a week, let the graces flow upon you. Daily visits are even better. Receiving Jesus Christ truly and physically in Holy Communion (John 6:27-72) is the best way to express your love to God, Whom we are all called to love with our whole hearts, minds, souls, bodies, and all our strength. There is no better way to build up our treasure in Heaven.

If you have a hard time with this, then ask Mother Mary to help you. She will. If someone asks, "Why do you need Mary?" Find out if they have a spiritually blurred vision of Jesus Christ present in the Eucharistic Covenant. The Bible says Mary's soul "magnifies the Lord." (Luke 1:46) As a magnifying glass helps us to see things more clearly, so too the Blessed Mother will help us to more clearly see Jesus in the Eucharist. Do not be afraid to embrace Jesus with childlike confidence. You will make mistakes, but with the grace and mercy of God, you will grow. Remember, "Love takes time."

7. LOVE JESUS

These are the times of the "Triumph of the Immaculate Heart of Mary." What is the Triumph? Jesus said, "You are the salt of the earth. But what good is the salt if it goes flat? It is good for nothing except to be trodden on upon the ground." (Matthew 5:13) Flat salt is impure salt. Isn't that the problem with the world today? We don't love Jesus with pure hearts. Our Lady's messages will help purify your heart, so you can experience the love that God wants to give your soul. The Triumph is when Mary helps us love God the way She does: with Her whole heart, mind, soul, body, and all Her strength.

Overcome all your temptations with love. Always ask God for the grace to love Him so much that you will be so preoccupied and consumed with the fire of His love, that frustrations, temptations, and distractions will seem trivial.

Spiritual exercises of the soul will help you with this love. As a starting point, always beg God for the grace that the three powers of the soul: 1. The Memory, 2. The Intellect, 3. The Will, will be for the greater glory of God. These graces that God will give you will help you to grow in that love. Visit www.medj1.com.

See the book: *Angels of the Last Days.*

Once again, Our Lady is "full of grace," and God is using Her to give us this grace to grow in love.

CHAPTER THIRTEEN –
THE ROSARY PRAYER

The Rosary is a gift from Heaven that combines both the vocal prayer of the "Our Father" and the "angelic salutation to Mary" along with fifteen/twenty meditations on the Gospel lives of Jesus and Mary. Meditations on each of the twenty mysteries are accomplished during one "Our Father," ten "Hail Marys," and one "Glory Be." This is called a decade.

God designed the Rosary in a special way, so it could be said both individually, among families, and with larger groups. Vocal prayer can be shared with children and adults. However, the Holy Spirit can speak to each person individually and reveal the mystery during the meditation in the Gospel lives of Jesus and Mary. The Holy Spirit enables spiritual giants and beginners to bear much fruit, as they pray the Rosary together.

When someone is faced with the challenge of learning and praying the Rosary, oftentimes he or she asks the question: "Can't I just talk to God in my own words instead?" To answer this question adequately, five truths need to be understood about the Rosary:

I.   God asked us to pray the Rosary and has promised
     great rewards to those souls who respond.

II. It is a simple school to grow spiritually and to become
     a saint.

III. It is "The Weapon" against Satan.

IV. It is a superior form of mental prayer in which we learn
     about the lives of Jesus and Mary and also how to "live life
     with the living God."

V.   It is a very helpful way to learn about Holy Communion
     (Eucharist) and to prepare us to receive Holy Communion
     –the fruit from the Tree of Life and our Covenant with God.

Jesus Christ, the Son of God, taught us both by word and example
to pray. Saint Paul wrote, "Pray without ceasing and in all things
give thanks." (1 Thessalonians 5: 17-18) The Rosary is an effec-
tive tool to help us pray.

CHAPTER FOURTEEN -

I. THE FIRST TRUTH: GOD ASKED US TO PRAY THE ROSARY, AND HAS PROMISED GREAT REWARDS TO THOSE SOULS WHO RESPOND

The Bible points out in numerous places that God uses angels, saints, and men/women (prophets) to deliver His message to us. A good example is found in the Second Joyful Mystery of the Rosary–The Visitation of Mary to Elizabeth. Elizabeth was filled with the Holy Spirit, and said to Mary, "Blessed are You that have believed, because those things shall be accomplished that were spoken to You by the Lord." (Luke 1:45) This message is credited to the Lord, since it is He who sent the Angel Gabriel to speak these words to Mary. In these days, God is sending a message to us through Mary, the Queen of Angels. For people who respond the way Mary did, the scriptural message still applies: "Blessed are you who have believed." (Luke 1:45)

The Rosary prayer is a special gift from God, given to St. Dominic through the virginal hands of the Blessed Virgin Mary as an antidote to the ills of the Church and the whole world.

Several popes and saints who have commented on the Rosary recognize St. Dominic as have been given the Rosary by Our Lady. In addition, they all proclaim the power and effectiveness of this prayer. Some examples of these documents include:

1. *The Secret of the Rosary*, by Saint Louis DeMontfort.

2. Apostolic letter of Pope Pius IX, *Postquam Deo monente* (April 12, 1867).

3. Encyclical letter of Pope Leo XIII, *Supremi apostolatus* (September 1, 1883).

4. Letter of Pope Pius X, *Nivimus exiturum* (June 27, 1908).

5. Encyclical letter of Pope Benedict XV, *Fausto appetentedie* (June 29, 1921).

(Encyclical Letters can be obtained from the Daughters of Saint Paul, Chicago, IL and on the Internet).

The Devil with his many tricks has often tried to discourage the faithful from praying the Rosary. Without giving his arguments any validity, one fact is clear: there has not been one pope, saint, or Council of the Church that has ever proclaimed anything contrary to the Church's belief:

1. St. Dominic was given the Rosary by the Blessed Virgin Mary.

2. The Rosary is a powerful prayer that is very beneficial to our souls, and showers graces on others.

3. The Rosary is "The Weapon" against the Devil.

In fact, more popes have confirmed the apparition of Our Lady to Saint Dominic than any other (apparition) private revelation in the history of the Catholic Church.

Chapter 12 of the Book of Revelations clearly shows a battle between St. Michael the Archangel, along with "the Woman", Mother Mary, and Her children on Jesus' side against the Devil and the Devil's children.

Church teaching explains in more detail Blessed Mary's role as the "Woman." In *Evangelium Vitae, #103,* by Pope John Paul II, and *Signum Magnum* ("the sign") by Pope Paul VI, both popes describe Mary as the "New Eve" and "Mother of the Living." Christians rejoice at being called "brother of Jesus" and "children of Mary," while the demons are infuriated by this. In Revelations 12:13, the Devil persecutes the Woman because he was angry against Her; he goes on to make war with the rest of Her children who keep the commandments of God and have the testimony of Jesus Christ. (Revelations 12:17)

If you happen to be a person who separates themselves from or even attacks Marian devotion, ask yourself: "Whose side do I want to be on?"

Do not despair. Repent! Even Saint Joseph, a just man, thought Mary was guilty. He decided to divorce Her quietly because he did not understand the Incarnation of Christ. Fortunately, he listened to the messenger from Heaven and changed his mind. (Matthew 1:19-20) The innocent are always blamed. She is as innocent today as She was 2,000 years ago, and the Mother of God is still the faithful Handmaid of the Lord. We need to change our attitude as Saint Joseph did and make Her an important part of our lives.

Man's way of thinking often differs from God's way. It seems that the more the Rosary is downplayed by universities and society, the more God sends Our Lady to reassure us of its effectiveness.

In most of all the hundreds of apparitions around the world, including those at Lourdes, Fatima, and Medjugorje, the "Woman clothed with the sun" (Revelations 12:1) is asking us to pray the Rosary in order to bring God's grace upon mankind and as a weapon against Satan.

Both St. Dominic, who founded the Dominican Order of Preachers, and Blessed Allen, O.P., received from Heaven "Fifteen Promises" to all who pray the fifteen decades of the Rosary daily. A little sample of some of these promises include:

#2. "I promise my special protection and the greatest graces to all those who shall recite the Rosary."

#3. "The Rosary shall be a powerful armor against hell. It will destroy vice, decrease sin, and defeat heresy."

#11. "You shall obtain all you ask of Me by the recitation of the Rosary."

God is good, and He makes His doctrine easy for us by giving Jesus and Mary as living examples. Do not be afraid of achieving a more personal relationship with Jesus. Every Christian acknowledges that the number one commandment is to love God with all our hearts, minds, souls, and bodies. No one loved Jesus Christ, the second person of the Holy Trinity, as much as His Mother Mary did. When praying the Rosary, Our Lady teaches us how to know, love, and serve the Baby Jesus in the Joyful Mysteries, Jesus as the light of the world in the Luminious Mysteries, the crucified Jesus as redeemer of the world in the Sorrowful Mysteries, and the glorified and triumphant Jesus in the Glorious Mysteries.

When praying the Joyful Mysteries with your heart, you literally "live Christmas." During the Luminious Mysteries you "walk with Jesus" as He shines the Heavenly Light. During the Sorrowful Mysteries, you live Good Friday in which God gives a living example of the commandment: "There is no greater love than this, to lay down one's life for one's friends." (John 15:13) Praying the Glorious Mysteries, you live Easter Sunday when Jesus opened the gates of Heaven, and Pentecost Sunday when the Holy Spirit, the Third Person of the Blessed Trinity, comes to guide the Church to the end of the world. Moreover, you reflect on the reward that "those who love Him" will receive at the end of their lives. As you pray/live the mysteries of Jesus and Mary, your heart opens, and you become aware of the truth that Jesus and Mary are alive and working in your life also.

Remember, it is God Who sends His messengers, Mary, Queen of Angels, angels, and prophets, with His message. When we respond to Our Lady's request to pray the Rosary given at Lourdes, Fatima, and Medjugorje, we are responding to God.

CHAPTER FIFTEEN -
II. THE SECOND TRUTH: THE ROSARY IS A SIMPLE SCHOOL TO GROW SPIRITUALLY AND BECOME A SAINT

Talking to God is good, but God wants more from you. In addition to conversing with God during the Rosary and the Mass, you can also talk to Him in your own words. The spiritual life is a school in which we learn from God. A child may say, "I want to learn about art, but I have no use for reading, math, and science." Good parents will strongly encourage the child to attend a school that teaches all of these. It will make the child more balanced as he grows and prepares Him for his future life. Similarly, our good Heavenly Father and Mother strongly encourage us to attend the school of praying the Rosary, attending Mass, reading the Bible, and talking to God in your own words. They know it will best prepare your soul for this life and the afterlife. Limiting yourself only to talking with God in your own words results in a lack of spiritual growth and a shallow relationship with Him. If we just talk to God, our fallen nature may reduce the quality of our conversation to: "Dear God, please give me that new red car with the big engine..." However, after meditating upon the Christmas scene, our conversation will become: "Dear God, please help me

to appreciate the precious time, peace, and joy with the loved ones
You gave me, no matter where we end up."

STRENGTH FROM REPETITION:

Repetition can be a good thing. Jesus told us not to use "vain
repetition" when we pray. The Devil tries to interpret "vain repetition" to mean "repetition" in an effort to break our union with
God. Similarly, if a mother tells Her children not to use a "broken
glass" when they drink, and if they misinterpret this as not to use
a "glass" to drink, they may go thirsty. "Vain" and "broken" are
the things to avoid, not "repetition" or "glass."

If you do not pray with your heart, it becomes vain repetition. If
you pray with your heart, it is an expression of love. How many
times can a couple in love repeat the words "I love you"? The
angels in Heaven are repeatedly saying, "Hosanna" and "Holy,
Holy, Holy Lord" to praise God. (Revelation 4:8)

Sometimes it takes humility to repeat a prayer, but do not worry,
in the spiritual world, humility is a good thing: "He that humbles
himself shall be exalted." (Matthew 23:12) Also, the *New Catechism* states, "Humility is the foundation of prayer."(#2559)

Repetition with the heart is a spiritual exercise by which the soul
can grow in virtue. To the soul, the difference between knowledge of the Rosary and praying it is like the difference between
knowing how to do a "push up" and doing three sets of fifty every
day. If you take either exercise seriously, you will know that they
have to be done every day for the best results. Even basketball
superstars have to repeat shooting several free throws every day
to stay on top of their game.

Exercise builds strength. Knowledge is not the problem in the
world. We know the Ten Commandments, but we do not have the
strength to follow them. The Rosary will help us acquire grace to
build up this strength in our souls.

DIFFICULTY IN PRAYING

Prayer is not only something we give to God, it is a gift from God. Saint Paul wrote, "We are many members of one body, the body of Christ." (1 Corinthians 12:20, 27) Just as blood nourishes the members of the body, prayer nourishes our soul. Do the members of the body give the heart blood? The blood circulates through the members and back to the heart. The blood comes from the heart with gifts filled with oxygen and nutrients. Prayer comes from God with the seven gifts of the Holy Spirit: wisdom, understanding, council, fortitude, knowledge, piety, and fear of the Lord. (Isaiah 11:2-3)

As the blood provides nourishment so that the members of the body can grow and function, so prayer provides the gifts of the Holy Spirit, so that our souls can grow and bear the twelve fruits of the Holy Spirit. They include: love, joy, peace, patience, kindness, faith...and chastity. (Galatians 5:22)

Blood is life and keeps the members united with the heart. Prayer is life for our souls and keeps us united with God.

So if prayer is so good, why is it so difficult?

It is the Holy Will of God that the blood flows from the heart to the members, and it is also the will of God that prayer flows from God through our hearts and back to God.

To "not pray" is to cause a blockage in this flow. There are two kinds of blockages. The first type of blockage can be experienced by sitting in an awkward position. The blood circulation to your feet can get cut off. Upon standing up, the pain of "pins and needles" is felt as the blood is once again circulated to your feet. If you begin praying again, you may feel the "pins and needles" of the soul as the Holy Spirit starts passing through you. This can be difficult at first, but it is important to persevere. Our Blessed Mother says, "Pray and one day prayer will become a joy for you."

The second kind of blockage is more severe. If the body suffers a stroke, it can become partially or totally paralyzed. Sometimes the damage is permanent. Other times, with therapy, exercise, and circulation, it regains its function. One could look at the whole Church as if we had had a stroke. Only some of the members move forward to God, and then slowly drag along the paralyzed members. The Blessed Mother's "Peace Plan" of Medjugorje will give us the therapy, exercise, and circulation we need to restore fully, wholly, and healthy the Body of Christ.

Responding with love to "pray, pray, pray" will bring health back to our souls and strength back to our Church.

PROMOTES CONVERSION

The Rosary changes lives and hearts. The first noticeable difference in my own life became apparent when I accidentally struck my finger with a hammer. Before, if this happened, as a reflex, I would swear and even curse God. Upon meditating on the passion of Jesus, often, one thinks about how it must have felt for the nails to go through His hands and feet. When pain was inflicted on my finger, as a reflex, instead of cursing, I thought of Jesus' passion and my heart said, "Wow, does Jesus love us!"

This reflex is very important because Our Mother Mary stresses the importance of being united with God at the hour of our death. What would happen if our death was painful, and we found ourselves before the throne of Almighty God cursing Him?

OVERCOMING DISTRACTIONS

A large section of the *New Catechism* is titled the "Battle of Prayer" (#2725): "We have to overcome ourselves and the tempter who does all he can to turn man away from prayer, away from union with God."

If we make prayer a priority, then through prayer God will work in us and with us. If we do not maintain union with God, our fallen nature and the tempter will have us working for Mammon or the Devil. How do birds know to fly south for the winter? God lets them know. Similarly, God will provide us with inspiration on how to focus our work and efforts.

Distractions can interfere with our prayer lives and lead to our frustration and eventually abandonment of prayer. Personally, over the years, I have struggled very much with distractions. Struggles can help keep one humble and can be a positive learning experience.

Some things I find helpful to overcome these distractions include:

1. Keep asking God for the grace of prayer.

2. Wear a blessed object, especially the brown scapular of Our Lady.

3. Oftentimes, pray the Rosary with the scriptures to fill your memory with information that the Holy Spirit can draw upon.

4. During difficult days, pray in front of a crucifix and focus your eyes on the face of Jesus. If you keep your eyes on Jesus, your mind will follow. Fold your hands in a reverent attitude of prayer and graces will flow.

5. Offer your prayers for Our Lady's intentions. At times you may think that prayers do not do any good. Since Our Lady asks so often for prayers, one is sure that they are very valuable to Her. Oftentimes, this will provide motivation, because the soul knows it is good to please its Queen.

During a practice game, a golfer will have someone jingle keys in an attempt to break his concentration. By struggling to overcome this distraction in practice, the golfer develops greater concentration skills. In the same way, a person who overcomes distractions in prayer will be more skilled at concentrating on God.

CHAPTER SIXTEEN -
III. THE THIRD TRUTH: THE ROSARY IS THE WEAPON AGAINST SATAN

As discussed earlier, the Rosary as "The Weapon," is foreshadowed in the Old Testament with the sling David used against Goliath. (1 Samuel 17 or 1 Kings 17, Douay version) Hold a Rosary by the cross and swing it around, and you will see David's sling. When Goliath defied the armies of the living God, and the King promised that he would give the one who could defeat him: (1 Samuel 17:25)

1. Great riches.

2. His daughter.

3. Freedom of tributes in the land.

The "15 promises" given to those who pray the Rosary fulfill the king's promises:

(1) #10. (Great riches) "The faithful children of the Rosary shall merit a high degree of glory in Heaven."

(2) #14. (God the Father's special daughter is Mary) "All who recite the Rosary are My sons and daughters, and brothers and sisters of My Son, Jesus Christ."

(3) #9. (Freedom of tributes in the land) "I shall deliver from Purgatory those who have been devoted to the Rosary."

The king's promises on earth to David foreshadows God's promises to us in Heaven.

Our Lady calls us to pray, pray, pray, and practice, practice, practice.

When David volunteered to fight Goliath, Saul said, "You are just a boy. This guy is a warrior. How can you beat him?" David explained how he had been practicing with his sling. While defending his father's sheep, he killed both a lion and a bear with the help of God, and Goliath, he claimed, would be like one of them. (Samuel 17:32-37)

The New Testament shows a battle between "The Woman clothed with the sun," (Mother Mary) Her children, and Saint Michael the Archangel on one side, and the Serpent or Devil and his demons on the other side. If you are not sure that this Woman is Mary, then join the 20 million people a year who visit the miraculous image of "Our Lady of Guadalupe" outside of Mexico City. Even scientists from NASA were allowed to perform infrared test work on the image to prove its miraculous nature. In this image, Mary is clothed with the sun, with the moon under Her feet, just as the scriptures describe Her. The miracle of the image of Our Lady of Guadalupe initiated the greatest conversion event in history. This image was the major tool for converting eight million Aztecs from worshipping their god – the Old Stone Serpent – with human sacrifices, to embracing Jesus Christ, the Second Person of the Blessed Trinity of the one true God. For more information on this ("Post card from Heaven") read the book: *Wonders of*

Guadalupe (Tan publishers, Rockford, IL, 1-800-437-5876).

In Revelations 13, another beast is described as similar to what David fought. The Beast was a combination of a leopard, bear, and lion and blasphemed and defied the army of the living God. Goliath prefigures the anti-Christ who is the Devil. In Revelations 20, an angel is described with a great chain in his hand that binds the Devil and casts him into a bottomless pit. Our Lady let us know that the great chain in his hand consists of the Rosaries that we pray.

Before David fought Goliath, Saul's attendants tried to dress him with their armor of conventional weapons. David had to take them off because they weighed him down. (Samuel 17:38-39) Similarly, many people offer alternative advice on how to fight the evils of today, but these are just going to weigh you down.

David grabbed his shepherd's staff, the sling, and five smooth stones, and rushed out to meet Goliath. The five smooth stones represent the five decades of the Rosary. When Goliath saw the boy, he was furious. "What am I, a dog that you come at me with a stick?" David replied, "You come to me with a sword, a spear, and a shield, but I come to you in the name of the Lord of hosts." (Samuel 17:40-45)

The key to the effectiveness comes from the kinetic energy of the stone and its direction. The key to the power of the Rosary, when prayed with the heart, is Love with our hearts directed towards Jesus. When praying the Rosary with the heart, Mother Mary will teach you how to love the Baby Jesus, love the Crucified Jesus, and love the Glorified Jesus. Since this helps fulfill the most important commandment, (i.e., to love God), the God Who is Love will take care of all our problems with His infinite power.

If you ask, "Why the Rosary?" look at what David said about why he used the sling: "All the assembly will know that God does not save with the sword and spear. FOR IT IS HIS BATTLE, and he will deliver you into our hands." (Samuel 17:47)

David strikes Goliath in the forehead with the first stone. The fruit of the First Mystery, the Annunciation, is humility. God is going to use the humility of the Blessed Mother to crush the proud head of Satan. One of the oldest prophecies in the Bible is Genesis 3:15. God said to the serpent, "I will put enmities between you and the Woman, between your seed (children) and Her seed. She will crush your head, and you will lie in wait of Her heel."

On Saturday, November 27, in the year 1830, God gave Saint Catherine Laboure of rue du Bac Paris, the vision of the Immaculate Conception. The Immaculate Conception means that God put enmities between Mary and the Devil. (Genesis 3:15) Heaven asked St. Catherine to make a medal of the vision in which "She," Mary, crushes the head of the serpent. God confirmed the importance of this vision depicted on the medal. Many miracles happened through it, that its name was changed to the Miraculous Medal. God has ways of letting us know how to highlight certain Biblical passages. God also preserved St. Catherine's body. After 125 years, her body is incorrupt and can be viewed in a glass coffin. She is the only incorrupt saint who has her eyes open, which is a spectacular miracle. You can see her body in Paris, on 140 rue du Bac, at the Miraculous Medal Shrine.

HISTORIC BATTLES

When the Muslims threatened to invade and wipe out Christianity in Europe, the strategic naval battle of Lepanto took place on Sunday, October 7, 1571. Although the Muslim Turks greatly outnumbered the Christian Spanish fleet, Pope Pius V called for the people of the Church to pray the Rosary as a last resort to help with the battle. During the battle, the wind shifted several times so that the Muslim boats kept colliding with each other. The

Spanish boats won with one of the greatest naval upsets in history. The Church commemorates the event by celebrating October 7 as the feast of the Holy Rosary, or Our Lady of Victory.

The sooner we devoutly pray the Rosary, the sooner all spiritual enemies will be overcome.

PRAY SLOW WITH THE HEART

Our Lady has asked us many times to pray the Rosary slowly with our heart. Pray with reverence, devotion, love, and meditate on its mysteries. To get a feel for the pace, imagine that you are the Angel Gabriel and God sent you to deliver the first "Hail Mary." Record the time it takes you to say this to Her. During public apparitions when Our Lady asked us to pray slowly, I timed the Hail Marys of which she said, "There, that is good." The time was 23-24 seconds per Hail Mary. Be patient. Be generous with your time given to God. Part of the battle is to "overcome ourselves." With love, you will do it. If the Hail Mary is an expression of love to your Heavenly Mother, the extra time spent will bring peace and joy to your soul.

CHAPTER SEVENTEEN -
IV. THE FOURTH TRUTH: THE ROSARY IS A SUPERIOR FORM OF MENTAL PRAYER

The ultimate goal of mental prayer is to live life with the living God.

In the early 1200's, St. Dominic fought the Albigensian heresy, which taught that all flesh is bad. He was very unsuccessful for many years until Our Lady gave him the Rosary. When the faithful started to pray the Rosary and learned to meditate, they understood that "The Word was made flesh and dwelt among us." (John 1:14) Baby Jesus was flesh, and the Baby Jesus was good. Therefore, not all flesh is bad.

When people do not know how to meditate, they become a vacuum for bad ideas or heresies. With mental prayer, they naturally reject errors, and the Holy Spirit helps them.

At the time that the errors and heresies were spreading throughout Europe, Dominic's Order of Preachers began teaching mental prayer through the Rosary, and it grew in numbers at a miraculous rate. God was showering countless miracles on the faithful to encourage them to learn mental prayer.

The Rosary provides the tools necessary not only to learn about Jesus, but to live with Jesus.

To meditate on the mysteries of the Rosary, one must use the three powers of the soul: the memory, the intellect, and the will.

1. The Memory – in which you recall the subject and ask questions such as: WHAT? What do I see? What do I hear? What do I smell? What do I feel?

2. The Intellect – in which you reflect, think about, and analyze the subject, by asking questions such as WHY?

3. The Will – in which you make a resolution to improve your life.

Make the statement "I WILL TRY..."

Within its section on meditation, the *New Catechism of the Catholic Church* states that Christian prayer should try, above all, to meditate on the mysteries of Christ as shown in the Rosary (#2708).

At first, these steps may seem difficult. The first steps to driving a car may also seem difficult. There are many details to worry about: "What gear do I put the car in? How much gas do I give it? There are pedestrians walking in front of me. It is raining out, etc." After some practice, these concerns become easy to handle and even fun.

As your soul spends time meditating on the lives of Jesus and Mary, you will grow spiritually and be able to see Jesus and Mary at work in your life. This is how to achieve mental prayer's ultimate goal of "living life with the living God."

The Rosary is a powerful form of mental prayer. To plunge deeper into the mysteries, the "Spiritual Exercises" of Saint Ignatius of Loyola are highly recommended.

Also, for more inspiration and insights into the Rosary, I would recommend reading Saint Louis DeMontfort's *Secret of the Rosary*. (Montfort Fathers, Bayshore, NY, 11706-8993 or call TAN 1-800-437-5876)

For more information on mental prayer, contact the lay apostolate of the *"Angels of the Last Days"* on the Internet (www.medj1.com). Angel members learn how to meditate and then teach others how to meditate. The constitution consists of many biblical stories of angels, which Angel members watch, listen to, and imitate the angel. As they do this, they pick up the principles of mental prayer. To become an Angel member, they take a vow:

"Dear God, I promise to beg You to please give me the grace that the three powers of my soul – my memory, my intellect, and my will – will be for the greater glory of God."

SCRIPTURAL ROSARY

In Saint Louis DeMontfort's Consecration, he points out that the "Teaching of Christ is greater than the advice of all the saints taken together...Unfortunately, however, so many people care little or nothing about the word of God." (Twenty-ninth day of "Total Consecration")

The word of God will give much power to your Rosaries and will help you with your meditations. As St. Jerome said, "To be ignorant of the scriptures is to be ignorant of Christ." However, when most people try to read the Bible, they find it difficult and overwhelming to read, and just give up. The New Testament fulfills everything in the Old Testament. Imagine a plant. The roots, stem, and leaves are the Old Testament, and the beautiful flower is the New Testament. Heaven picks out the best 15/20 mysteries from the Gospel lives of Jesus and Mary, to make the Bible easy for us to understand.

The Devil tempts Jesus in the desert by quoting the Bible. Jesus resists the temptation by showing that the scripture passage is taken out of context. (Matthew 4:6-7)

With the fifteen/twenty mysteries of the Rosary, Heaven gives us a panoramic view of the scriptures, including the Incarnation of Christ in the womb of Mary, His public life, His death, Resurrection, Ascension and the Glorification of the elect. When the "big picture" is understood, the temptation of taking Scripture out of context is more easily overcome.

FAITH AND REASON

Before going to Medjugorje, I believed in and loved God, the Father Almighty, Creator of Heaven and Earth. It was everything else in the Creed that totally confused me. Grace and reason led me to know that there is a God. Created objects have an "order" that requires intelligence and power. Engineers can use their intelligence to design and build a bridge out of steel, concrete, and cable. If one were to just randomly throw these ingredients together, the result would not be a bridge, but a mess. People can marvel at the creation of the bridge and congratulate the engineers who designed it. It takes intelligence and power to provide the "order" found in the bridge's creation.

What would happen if Harry built a very nice room addition onto his house and his family said, "The plaster, wood, tile and wires just fell together and that is how it came out?"

What would happen if Kay spent two years on a detailed painting of a panda bear and her family said, "That paint and canvas fell together by chance and made that image?" Would Harry and Kay be offended?

Ninety-five percent of our human bodies consist of four elements: carbon, hydrogen, oxygen, and nitrogen. For example, take a glass half filled with water (hydrogen, oxygen), and add the inside of a pencil to it (carbon). The resulting mixture with the air (nitrogen), contains the same four elements of which human beings consist. If these ingredients were randomly thrown together, the results would not be a person, but a mess. A human being is extremely more complicated than anything man can conceive. This "Divine Order" takes Divine Intelligence and power. People can marvel at the beauty of creation and are obliged to congratulate the God who designed and made it.

Actually, if anyone expected me to believe that a bridge, a room addition, a painting, or a human body just came together by itself, it would be an insult to my intelligence.

On meditating on all the perfect details in the "home" or earth that God has made and given to us, grace and reason let me know that not only does God exist, but also that He loves us.

Chemistry formulas are intended to help people use elements in the world to create products that serve mankind. The formulas in religion are intended by God to help people know, love, and serve Him better and to reach our goal of Heaven after our earthly journey.

Our purpose in life can be lived out more deeply when we use the formulas of religion that we learn while praying the Scriptural Rosary. Christmas shows us that God is not only out in space somewhere, but also with us. We can hug God, and He can hug us. We can serve God, and He can serve us. We can grow and live with the living God and He will give us great rewards in Heaven. Why cheat yourself out of these good formulas? God wants us to use them and to share them with others.

Applying the correct formulas of gasoline allows our cars to take us where we want to go. In a similar way, applying the correct formulas of religion can bring us to great treasures for eternity. I learned the truth of these formulas while praying the Scriptural Rosary.

With grace and reason, I came to believe that Jesus Christ is Lord. Jesus Christ is both true God and true man. Jesus is the Way, the Truth, and the Life. Without Jesus, we would be lost in both this world and the next. With Jesus, we have everything.

BIBLE LESSONS

In the Bible, God reveals Himself to us, and also reveals "us to us." By meditating with the scriptures, many of the "whys" and "hows" of day-to-day living will be revealed.

If you make it a habit to do at least one of your fifteen/twenty mysteries a day, with the Scriptures, it will make all your other Rosaries more fruitful. If you get rooted in the Word of God, then the Holy Spirit will draw nourishment from your soul's memory into the intellect and heart, even when praying the mysteries without the Scriptures present. This will happen similar to a tree that draws nourishment from its roots even when it is not raining.

Look at the incredible three-and-one-third year pace in which Jesus taught His Apostles, who were only fishermen, everything. It must have been very difficult for them to remember so much. However, they were rooted in the Word of God, and Jesus promised that the Holy Spirit would help them remember. The same thing will happen to you by praying the Scriptural Rosary.

The *New Catechism* states that the Old Testament prepares us for the New Testament, and the New Testament helps us to understand the Old. Good examples of this are found while meditating on the 15/20 mysteries of the Rosary.

Christians, Muslims, and Jews all respect the importance of Abraham who was willing to sacrifice his only son to prove his love to God (Genesis 22). However, the Christian sees this also as a preparation for the fulfillment in which God the Father proves His Love to us by sacrificing His only Son. When meditating, we see that the son

Isaac, had to climb up the hill with the wood on his back to reach the place of sacrifice. The Christian sees the story of Issac fulfilled in Jesus, carrying the wood of the Cross up Calvary. Abraham said, "God Himself will provide the victim for the sacrifice," and at the top of Mt. Moriah, he and Issac found a ram with its head caught in some thorns. Two-thousand years later, John the Baptist called Jesus the "Lamb of God who takes away the sins of the world." Then, during His passion, Jesus had a "crown of thorns" placed on His head. The similarity becomes even more amazing when noting that the physical location of Jesus' sacrifice on Calvary is extremely close to Mount Moriah, the spot where Abraham intended to offer his sacrifice.

This type of foreshadowing takes place throughout the entire Bible. The Old Testament is like looking at a shadow of an ice cream cone, the New Testament is looking at the actual ice cream cone, and living your Catholic faith with the living God is like eating the ice cream cone. The Rosary bridges the gap to help you live the faith.

53 HAIL MARYS, 53 DAYS

God became man to be part of human history. Jesus Christ is the center of human history. Jesus said, "I did not come to destroy the law or the prophets, but to fulfill." (Matthew 5:17) Jesus Christ fulfilled all the scriptures in the short 33-1/3 years He lived on earth. Nine of the 20 mysteries take place in a 53-day period. When one meditates on how many prophecies from scripture were fulfilled in these 53 days, reason says, only the power of God could do such a thing.

The Rosary will help with conversion. Consider the conversion that St. Peter had over the 53 most remarkable days in the history of mankind. One of the many highlights is Holy Thursday, when Jesus established the New and Everlasting Covenant with His people, by giving us the "True Bread from Heaven." In the Old Testament, Moses led the Israelites through the desert and God fed them with bread from Heaven. Now, in the Eucharist, Jesus gives Himself as food for our souls to strengthen us during our pilgrimage of life. He also fulfilled giving us the Fruit from the Tree of Life, and the Priesthood of Melchizedek, the King of Salem (Peace), who brought bread and wine to offer to God. (Genesis 14:18)

Also on Holy Thursday, Peter, who was very sure of his loyalty to Jesus, fell asleep in the Garden of Gethsemane when the Lord asked him to pray. Finally, after he and all the Apostles abandoned Jesus, Peter denied Jesus three times before the cock crowed, and ran out weeping bitterly. (Luke 22:61-62)

The second day is Good Friday, when Jesus gave us the ultimate example of, "No greater love than this to lay down ones life for his friends." (John 15:13) Many prophets in the Old Testament describe a suffering Messiah, a "Man of Sorrows." (Isaiah 53:3) On Passover, the Israelites sacrificed a lamb so that the angel of death would pass over them. Jesus fulfills the Passover, by truly becoming the Lamb of God who takes away the sins of the world. Actually, Jesus was crucified at the same time the sacrificial lambs were being killed for the Passover Supper. On the fourth day of the 53, Jesus raises Himself from the dead on Easter Sunday. The angel told Mary that Jesus would reign in the house of Jacob forever. Jacob's sons threw their brother, Joseph, into a pit to die, and then he was pulled out. As Joseph came out of the earth alive, Jesus came out of the tomb alive. He destroyed death to give us life and opened for us the Gates of Heaven. Peter and the others were still so much in shock that they were not too quick to believe that Jesus had risen.

Then, forty days after His Resurrection, Jesus gave the Apostles their final instructions; He asked Peter three times to feed His sheep, because there will be "one shepherd and one fold." (John 10:16) Jesus then ascended to Heaven to sit at the right hand of the Father, while the angels reminded His Disciples present and all of humankind that He will come again. Then Jesus' Disciples gathered together and prayed with Mary, His Mother, to prepare for the fulfillment of His promise. Jesus said that He would not leave us orphans. On the 53rd day, Pentecost Sunday, the third Person of the Blessed Trinity came down on the Church that Jesus had established to truly set the world on fire with the love of God. Happy birthday, "Bride of Christ."

It is incredible to meditate on how countless prophecies in both the Old and New Testament were fulfilled in this 53-day period. Look at Peter. He was filled with the Holy Spirit and became very bold. Fifty-three days before, this frightened fisherman ran away crying. After Pentecost, however, he was given the power to put the whole Sanhedrin on trial: "God has raised Jesus again, and we are His witnesses...God has made both Lord and Christ, this Jesus whom you have crucified." (Acts 2:32,36) To obtain the grace of conversion, pray the Rosary with the heart, and your soul will be enriched with a conversion like Peter's. You will live through those 53 Hail Marys as Peter lived through those 53 days. The Rosary is a gift from Heaven to fill us with the Holy Spirit, so we can live out our individual pilgrimages on earth.

ROSARY MYSTERIES AS BIBLE STUDY

Take time to look up the New and Old Testament passages in the Scriptural Rosary, and read the whole paragraph, or learn the entire story. This type of study will bear much fruit, and will be refreshed each time you pray the Rosary. The Bible has many levels to it, and God will reveal to you insights for your "day to day" life. It is like putting money in the Heavenly bank. Thank You, Jesus, for making it so easy to know, love, and serve You.

CHAPTER EIGHTEEN -
V. THE FIFTH TRUTH: THE ROSARY HELPS US TO UNDERSTAND JESUS, THE EUCHARIST, THE FRUIT FROM THE TREE OF LIFE

Remember, there were two special trees in the Garden of Eden. After Adam and Eve were driven out, all of humanity was destined to die. However, there was an antidote: "Unless he reach forth his hand and eat from the Tree of Life and live forever." (Genesis 3:22) The Lord cast Adam out of Paradise and placed a Cherubim (angel) and a flaming sword to keep the path of the Tree of Life. (Genesis 3:24) The Tree of Life is discussed also in the last chapter of the entire Bible. "I Am the Alpha and Omega, the First and the Last, the Beginning and the End. Blessed are they that wash their robes in the Blood of the Lamb, that they might have a right to the Tree of Life, and enter into the gates into the city." (Revelations 22:13-14)

In studying the Rosary Mysteries, the Joyful Mysteries show that Jesus' Mother, Mary, is the "Tree of Life." The Luminious Mysteries show that the Eucharist is the fruit from the Tree of Life. The Sorrowful Mysteries show that the Cross is the "Tree of Life." The Glorious Mysteries show that all members of the Church, particularly those of the Priesthood, are the "Tree of

Life." The fruit of all these is always Jesus Christ. Some clues to finding the "Tree of Life" are noted by an "*" in the following Scriptural Rosary.

For example, four clues that Mother Mary is the true Tree of Life are:

1. Her ways are beautiful ways, and all Her paths are peace. She is a tree of life to them that lay hold of Her: he that retains Her is blessed. (Proverbs 3:17-18)

2. And Elizabeth was filled with the Holy Spirit, and cried out with a loud voice, saying, "Blessed art thou among women and blessed is the fruit of Thy womb!" (Luke 1:42)

NOTE: The fruit of Mary's womb is Jesus Christ, the Son of God.

3. Jesus said, "I am the living Bread, which came down from Heaven. If any man shall eat this Bread, he shall live forever. And the Bread that I give is My Flesh for the life of the world...He that eats My Flesh and drinks My Blood has everlasting life and I will raise him up on the last day." (John 6:51,52,55)

NOTE: We have to eat the fruit from the Tree of Life and live forever. Jesus Christ comes to us in the form of living Bread or Holy Communion.

4. Jesus took bread, blessed and broke it, and gave it to His disciples, saying, "Take and eat; this is My Body." And taking a cup He gave thanks and gave it to them saying, "All of you drink of this. For this is My Blood of the new covenant, which is being shed for many unto the forgiveness of sins." (Matthew 26:26-28)

NOTE: Holy Communion is also the new and everlasting covenant with God.

SUMMARY:

Mary is the true Tree of Life, and the fruit of Her womb is Jesus Christ. We must eat the Living Bread and live forever. Most people said, "This saying is difficult," and left Jesus. (John 6:67) Our Lady of Medjugorje is doing a good job calling them back home.

The slavery of sin came into the world because Eve stole God's fruit and Adam's pride led to disobedience. To undo this damage and free us from eternal slavery, Jesus Christ, the "New Adam," humbled Himself, becoming obedient unto death, even to death on the Cross. (Philippians 2:8)

Mary, the "New Eve," had to give up the "Fruit of Her Womb," to make up for the fruit that Eve stole. Because this took place on Calvary, the Cross also becomes the Tree of Life. Jesus Christ, nailed to the Cross, is the Fruit from the Tree of Life that we must eat to live forever.

When we attend Holy Mass, the sacrifice at Calvary is made present. In a heroic way, Jesus offered Himself to the Father as a sacrifice on the altar of the Cross to save us. With the cost of His Blood, He purchases for us the opportunity for His Living Body to live in us. As we receive Communion, we eat the fruit from the Tree of Life and will live forever.

Because God uses the Church to give us Holy Communion, it is also the Tree of Life. The fruit we, as members of the Church, bear is Jesus Christ becoming alive in others. This is what evangelization is about. Because the Church is apostolic, the number twelve can be associated with the Tree of Life in the Bible.

The Eucharist is God's most powerful means of giving us a personal relationship with Jesus.

When eating the fruit of the "Tree of Life," do not be shocked at the tough words of Jesus: "Unless you eat the Flesh of the Son of Man and drink His blood, you have no life within you." (John 6:54) The Eucharist, however, is not dead flesh. Jesus is alive in Holy Communion and wants to live in you. How else can Jesus make it clear that IT IS NOT JUST A SYMBOL? It was truly His Flesh and Blood that was laid in the manger on that first Christmas Day. He truly felt the cold of the air and the warmth of His Mother's hug. It was truly His Flesh and Blood that was nailed to the Cross. It was truly His Flesh and Blood that resurrected and ascended into Heaven. It is the resurrected and glorified body of Jesus, that could enter a room, "though the doors were locked" (John 20:26) – which is the Eucharist.

Imagine that Jesus Christ wants your body to be His home, similar to how He lived inside the Blessed Virgin Mary. Imagine a throne is set on the altar of your heart. Imagine that Jesus Christ walks into a room and gives you a big hug. In doing so His glorified body goes right inside of yours and He sits on the throne of your heart. This is what happens during Holy Communion. Eating the Eucharist is the means God choses to accomplish this.

It is truly His Flesh and Blood that will be joined to yours in Holy Communion, and you two shall become one flesh. (Ephesians 5:32,33) What intimacy a God of love desires with His creatures!

The Church teaches that this union with mankind is the number one dogma of the faith. Everything else in the Church is directed toward it. (Canon Law #897) Imagine if 80% of the players on your football team do not know how important it is to score a touchdown. The confusion would make it easy for the opposing team to run up the score. Similarly, in our spiritual battle between good and evil, confusion caused by the lack of knowledge in the Covenant of the Eucharist allows the evil forces to create havoc in today's society.

Both Christians and Jews hold Moses in high esteem because he talked with God, face to face. On Mount Sinai, God said: "Take your shoes off, this is Holy Ground." (Exodus 3:5) Scripture states that God Himself not only talks to, but lives inside the Blessed Virgin Mary. This is a quantum leap from the experience of Moses to that of Mary. Christians learn from Mary because we are to experience this greater union with God. Mary will help us to receive God with love and intimacy because GOD HIMSELF PHYSICALLY LIVES IN US BY MEANS OF HOLY COMMUNION. Look at what we cost Him and embrace Jesus with the love He deserves; then receive everlasting life.

If we are not sure, how should we respond to Jesus in the Eucharist? Once again, pray the Rosary and look at Peter toward the end of the special 53 days. Peter and John were on a boat, and because of his spiritually blurred vision, Peter did not recognize Jesus. John evangelized to him saying, "It is the Lord." (John 21:7) Peter, with his whole heart, jumped into the lake in order to get closer to Jesus. Today, the Church, our Lady, and the angels, are evangelizing loud and clear: "It is the Lord!" So drop whatever you are doing, and plunge yourself closer to Jesus. As you get closer you will recognize the Lord just as Peter did.

CHAPTER NINTEEN
- PRAY, PRAY, PRAY

For over 25 years at Medjugorje, Our Lady has begged us to pray, pray, pray, for the condition of ourselves and of the world. Pray especially for young people, because the Devil has them in a difficult situation. Pray together as families, in prayer groups, and individually. You can even use Rosary video and audio-tapes to help. The Devil cannot defend himself against the Rosary. He can, however, discourage you from praying it. He is cunning and puts much effort into this discouragement. No matter what, DON'T BE AFRAID. Just like the Israelites were afraid of Goliath, many people today are ashamed of their faith because of all the present-day beasts that blaspheme God. Give time to the Rosary and make it a priority. Start today, and don't be afraid, because the "battle is the Lord's." Our Lady told us that the Devil is already starting to lose power, and God has revealed to us that, in the end, we will be victorious. The call is for you personally. Right now, pick up the Rosary in your hands and continue your conversion. Engage in fighting the good fight. As our Lady and Queen always says, "Thank you for having responded to My call."

FIRST JOYFUL MYSTERY: THE ANNUNCIATION

"Blessed are the meek and humble, they shall possess the land."
(Matthew 5:4)

"The angel Gabriel was sent from God to a town of Galilee called
Nazareth, to a Virgin betrothed to a man named Joseph, of the house
of David, and the Virgin's name was Mary. And when the angel
had come to Her, he said, 'Hail, full of grace, the Lord is with Thee.
Blessed art Thou among women.' When She had heard him She was
troubled at his word, and kept pondering what manner of greeting this
might be....and the angel said to Her, 'Do not be afraid, Mary, for thou
has found grace with God.'
(Luke 1:26-30); (Exodus 3:1-22)

FRUIT OF THE MYSTERY: HUMILITY

OUR FATHER

> *The first Scripture reference is the actual quote.*
> *The following references are for Bible study*
> *in light of the mystery.*

"Behold thou shall conceive in Thy womb and bring forth a Son; and
thou shall call Him Jesus." (Luke 1:31-32)
HAIL MARY

"He shall be great and shall be called the Son of the Most High. The
Lord God shall give Him the throne of David His father."
(Luke 1:32); (Isaiah 9:6-7)
HAIL MARY

"He shall reign in the house of Jacob forever, and of His kingdom
there shall be no end."
(Luke 1:32-33); (Daniel 6:25-27); (Daniel 7:10-15)
HAIL MARY

"Mary said to the Angel; 'How shall this be done, because I do not
know man?'" (Luke 1:34)
HAIL MARY

"The Angel said to Mary, 'The Holy Spirit shall come upon Thee and the power of the Most High shall overshadow Thee.'" (Luke 1:35); (Acts 2:1-4)
HAIL MARY

"Therefore the Holy One to be born shall be called the Son of God." (Luke 1:35); (Galatians 4:1-7)
HAIL MARY

"Elizabeth Your cousin also has conceived a son in her old age and she who was called barren is now in her sixth month; for nothing shall be impossible with God."
(Luke 1:36-37)
HAIL MARY

"Mary said, 'Behold the handmaid of the Lord; let it be done to Me according to thy word.'"
(Luke 1:38); (Daniel 14:8)
HAIL MARY

"And the Word was God....And the Word was made flesh, and dwelt among us." (John 1:1 & 1:14)
HAIL MARY

"Behold, the Virgin shall be with child, and shall bring forth a son; and they shall call His name Emmanuel which means, 'God with us.'" (Isaiah 7:14); (Matth. 1:23)
HAIL MARY

SECOND JOYFUL MYSTERY: THE VISITATION

"The one who serves the rest, is the greatest among you."
(Matthew 23:11)

"Mary arose and went with haste into the hill country, to a town of
Judah... When Elizabeth heard the greeting of Mary, the babe in her
womb leapt. And Elizabeth was filled with the Holy Spirit, and cried
out with a loud voice, saying, 'Blessed art thou among women and
blessed is the Fruit of thy Womb!* And how have I deserved that the
Mother of my Lord should come to me? For behold, the moment that
the sound of Thy greeting came to my ears, the babe in my womb leapt
for joy.' ...Mary stayed with her for three months (Luke 1:39-45,56);
(Jgs 5:24); (2Samuel 6:9-11); (Rom 15:7).

FRUIT OF THE MYSTERY: LOVE OF NEIGHBOR

OUR FATHER

"Before I formed you in the womb, I knew you."
(Jeremiah 1:5)
HAIL MARY

"Blessed is she who has believed."
(Luke 1:45); (Galatians 3)
HAIL MARY

"Mary said, 'My soul magnifies the Lord.'"
(Luke 1:46); (Psalms 34:4); (Romans 15:11)
HAIL MARY

"My spirit rejoices in God my Savior."
(Luke 1:47); (1Thes 5:16); (Psalms 34:9)
HAIL MARY

"Because He has regarded the humility of His Handmaid; for, behold
henceforth all generations shall call Me blessed."
(Luke 1:48); (Matthew 23:12)
HAIL MARY

"He that is mighty has done great things to Me. And Holy is His
name." (Luke 1:49); (1Pet 1:16); (Matt 6:9); (Lev 9:2)
HAIL MARY

"He has scattered the proud in the conceit of their heart.
He has exalted the humble." (Luke 1:51-52); (Isaiah 26:5)
HAIL MARY

"He has filled the hungry with good things."
(Luke 1:53); (Psalms 33:11); (1Samuel 2:5)
HAIL MARY

"Even as he spoke to our fathers-to Abraham and to his seed forever."
(Luke 1:55); (Genesis 17:7)
HAIL MARY

"Behold the tabernacle of God with men... and God himself with them,
shall be their God."
(Rev 21:3); (Exodus 40)
HAIL MARY

THIRD JOYFUL MYSTERY: THE BIRTH OF JESUS

"Blessed are the poor, for yours is the kingdom of God."
(Luke 6:20)

"Joseph...do not be afraid to take Mary for a wife...She has conceived
of the Holy Spirit." (Matthew 1:20)

"A decree went forth from Caesar Augustus that a census of the
whole world should be taken. And Joseph also went to the town of
David, which is called Bethlehem - to register, together with Mary
his espoused wife, Who was with Child... while they were there
She brought forth Her firstborn Son, and wrapped Him in swaddling
clothes, and laid Him in a manger, because there was no room for them
in the inn." (Luke 2:1-7); (Micheas 5:2); (Wisdom 7:3-5)

FRUIT OF THE MYSTERY: POVERTY

OUR FATHER
"The angel said to Joseph...'Call His name Jesus; for He shall save His
people from their sins." (Matthew 1:21)
HAIL MARY

"To the shepherds keeping night watch over their flock...the angel said;
'Do not be afraid, for behold, I bring you tidings of great joy, for today
a Savior has been born to you, who is Christ the Lord.'"
(Luke 2:8,11); (Isaiah 52:6-10)
HAIL MARY

"Suddenly there was with the angel a multitude of the heavenly host
praising God, and saying: 'Glory to God in the highest, and on earth
peace to men of good will.'"
(Luke 2:13-14)
HAIL MARY

"When the angels departed from them into heaven, the shepherds
went with haste and found Mary and Joseph, and the Babe lying in the
manger. And when they saw...they understood." (Luke 2:15-16)
HAIL MARY

"The Wise Men came from the East to Jerusalem, saying, 'Where is
He that is born King of the Jews? For we have seen His star in the
East and have come to worship Him.'"
(Matthew 2:2); (Psalm 72:10); (Numbers 24:17)
HAIL MARY

"Seeing the star, they rejoiced with great joy...They found the Child
with Mary His Mother, and falling down they worshipped Him...and
offered Him gifts: gold, frankincense, and myrrh."
(Matthew 2:10-11); (Isaiah 60:6)
HAIL MARY

"There will arise the Sun of Justice with its healing rays"
(Malachias 4:2).
"Jesus said, 'I am the Light of the world.'" (John 8:12);
(Isaiah 9:2); (2Machabees 1&2&10:1-8); (Genesis 1:3)
HAIL MARY

"Jesus said, 'I came that they might have life, and have it more abundantly.'" (John 10:10); (Exodus 30:15-20); (Genesis 1:20-31)
HAIL MARY

"They that received Him, He gave them power to be made the sons of
God." (John 1:12)
HAIL MARY

"Mary kept all these words, pondering them in Her heart."
(Luke 2:19); (Matthew 6:21)
HAIL MARY

FOURTH JOYFUL MYSTERY:
PRESENTATION OF JESUS IN THE TEMPLE

"I did not come to destroy the law or the prophets...but to fulfill."
(Matthew 5:17)

"And when the days of Her purification were fulfilled according to the
Law of Moses, they took (Jesus) up to Jerusalem to present Him to the
Lord - as it is written in the Law of the Lord, 'Every male that opens
the womb shall be called holy to the Lord' and to offer a sacrifice... a
pair of turtledoves." (Luke 2:21-24); (Exodus 13:2); (Leviticus 12:6);
(Hebrews 10:10-14)

FRUIT OF THE MYSTERY: OBEDIENCE

OUR FATHER

"Simeon was just and devout, and the Holy Spirit was upon him...He
took (the Child Jesus) into his arms." (Luke 2:25,28)
HAIL MARY

"Now Thou does dismiss Thy servant, O Lord, according to Thy word,
in peace; because my eyes have seen Thy
salvation." (Luke 2:29,30)
HAIL MARY

"Thou has prepared before the face of all peoples, a Light of revelation
to the Gentiles, and a Glory for Thy people Israel."
(Luke 2:32)
HAIL MARY

"Behold this Child is destined for the fall and the resurrection of many,
and for a sign that shall be contradicted."
(Luke 2:34); (Isaiah 8:14)
HAIL MARY

"(Mary), thy own soul a sword shall pierce, that the thoughts of many
hearts may be revealed."(Luke 2:35)
HAIL MARY

"Anna, a prophetess...was at the temple, serving night and day by fastings and prayers. She spoke of Him to all that looked for the redemption of Israel." (Luke 2:36-38)
HAIL MARY

"An Angel of the Lord appeared in sleep to Joseph saying, 'Arise and take the Child and His mother and flee into Egypt. Herod will seek the Child (Jesus) to destroy Him.'"
(Matthew 2:13); (Osee 11:1)
HAIL MARY

"Then Herod perceiving he was deluded by the wise men, was exceedingly angry and sending killed all the male children in Bethlehem... from two years old and younger."
(Matthew 2:16); (Jeremias 31:15)
HAIL MARY

"And the Child (Jesus) grew and became strong. He was full of wisdom and the grace of God was upon Him."
(Luke 2:40)
HAIL MARY

"For the Law was given through Moses; grace and truth came through Jesus Christ." (John 1:17)
HAIL MARY

FIFTH JOYFUL MYSTERY:
FINDING THE CHILD JESUS IN THE TEMPLE

"Blessed are they that weep and mourn, for they shall be comforted."
(Matthew 5:5); (Isaiah 61:2)

"His parents would go every year to Jerusalem at the Feast of the
Passover. And when He was twelve years old, as they were returning, the boy Jesus remained... and His parents did not know it. But
thinking that He was in the caravan, they had come a day's journey
before it occurred to them to look for (Jesus) among their relatives and
acquaintances. And not finding Him, they returned to Jerusalem in
search of Him." (Luke 2:41-45)

FRUIT OF THE MYSTERY: JOY IN FINDING JESUS

OUR FATHER

"As the hart thirsts for the fountains of water; so my soul thirsts after
Thee, O God." (Psalms 42:2)
HAIL MARY

"Ask and you shall receive, seek and you shall find, knock and it shall
be opened." (Matthew 7:7)
HAIL MARY

"After three days, they found (Jesus) in the temple, sitting in the midst
of the teachers, listening to them and asking them questions."
(Luke 2:46)
HAIL MARY

"All who were listening to (Jesus) were amazed at His answers."
(Luke 2:47)
HAIL MARY

"And His mother said to Him, 'Son why have You done this to us?
Behold in sorrow Thy father and I have been seeking Thee.'"
(Luke 2:48)
HAIL MARY

"'Did you not know that I must be about My Father's business?' And Jesus was subject to them." (Luke 2:50-51); (Exodus 20:12)
HAIL MARY

"Unless you become like this little child, you can not enter into the Kingdom of Heaven." (Matthew 18:17)
HAIL MARY

"And His mother kept all these things carefully in Her heart." (Luke 2:51); (Luke 12:34)
HAIL MARY

"And Jesus advanced in wisdom and age and grace before God and men." (Luke 2:52)
HAIL MARY

"The Word was made Flesh and dwelt among us, and we saw His glory." (John 1:14)
HAIL MARY

FIRST LUMINOUS MYSTERY:
THE BAPTISM OF JESUS

"John was in the desert, baptizing and preaching the baptism of penance, unto remission of sins. And there went out to him all the country of Judea and all they of Jerusalem and were baptized by him in the river of Jordan, confessing their sins... John was clothed in camel's hair and leather. He ate locusts and wild honey."
(Mark 1:2-6)

FRUIT: BECOMING CHILDREN OF GOD

OUR FATHER

John said, "I indeed baptize you in water unto penance, but He that shall come after me, is mightier than I, Whose shoes I am not worthy to bear: He shall baptize you in the Holy Spirit and fire."
(Matthew 3:11)
HAIL MARY

"The people asked; 'What shall we do?' John replied; 'He that has two coats give to him that has none.'"
(Luke 3:10-11)
HAIL MARY

"Jesus came from Galilee to the Jordan, unto John, to be baptized by him." (Matthew 3:13)
HAIL MARY

"But John resisted Him, saying: 'I ought to be baptized by You, and You come to me?' And Jesus answering, said to him: 'Let it be so now...to fulfill all justice.' "
(Matthew 3:14,15)
HAIL MARY

"And Jesus being baptized, came out of the water...the heavens were opened to Him: and he saw the Spirit of God descending as a dove, and it came upon Him."
(Matthew 3:16)
HAIL MARY

"And behold a voice from heaven saying: 'This is My beloved Son, in whom I am well pleased.'"
(Matthew 3:17)
HAIL MARY

"I will pour upon you clean water, and you shall be cleansed...I will give you a new heart, and put a new spirit within you...and you shall be My people, and I will be Your God." (Ezekiel 36:25-28)
HAIL MARY

Jesus answered, "Amen, amen I say to you, unless a man be born again of water and the Holy Ghost, he cannot enter the Kingdom of God." (John 3:5)
HAIL MARY

Jesus said, "He that believes and is baptized shall be saved, but he that believes not shall be condemned." (Mark 16:16)
HAIL MARY

"In the days of Noah, when the ark was being built, eight souls, were saved by water. Baptism...now saves you also." (1Peter 3:20-21)
HAIL MARY

SECOND LUMINOUS MYSTERY:
THE WEDDING FEAST AT CANA

"There was a marriage in Cana of Galilee: and the Mother of Jesus was there. Jesus and His disciples also were invited to the marriage. When the wine ran out, the Mother of Jesus said to Him: 'They have no wine.' And Jesus said to Her: 'Woman, what is that to Me and to Thee? My hour is not yet come.' His Mother said to the waiters, 'Do whatever He tells you.'" (John 2:1-5)

FRUIT: JESUS LOVES MARY

OUR FATHER

"Now there were six water-pots of stone, according to the manner of the purifying of the Jews, containing two or three measures apiece."
(John 2:6)
HAIL MARY

"Jesus said to them: 'Fill the water-pots with water.' And they filled them up to the brim." (John 2:7)
HAIL MARY

"Jesus said to them: 'Draw out now and carry to the chief steward of the feast.' And they carried it." (John 2:8)
HAIL MARY

"The chief steward had tasted the water made wine, not knowing where it came from, but the waiters who had drawn the water knew."
(John 2:9)
HAIL MARY

"The chief steward called the bridegroom, and said to him, 'Every man at first serves good wine, and after the men have been drinking, then a lesser vintage. But you have kept the good wine until now.'"
(John 2:10)
HAIL MARY

"This is the beginning of miracles that Jesus did in Cana of Galilee and He manifested His glory. And His disciples believed in Him."
(John 2:11)
HAIL MARY

"The Kingdom of Heaven is like a king who made a marriage feast for his son." (Matthew 22:2)
HAIL MARY

"A man shall leave his father and mother and cling to his wife, and the two shall become one flesh...What therefore God has joined together, let no man separate."
(Matthew 19:5-6)
HAIL MARY

"Let us be glad and rejoice and give glory to Him. For the marriage of the Lamb is come: and his wife has prepared herself."
(Revelations 19:7)
HAIL MARY

"Blessed are they that are called to the marriage supper of the Lamb. And he said to me, 'These words of God are true.'"
(Revelations 19:9)
HAIL MARY

THIRD LUMINOUS MYSTERY:
ANNOUNCEMENT OF THE KINGDOM

"For God so loved the world that He gave His only begotten Son, that those who believe in Him may not perish but have life everlasting." (John 3:16)

"Jesus came in Galilee, preaching the gospel of the kingdom of God. Jesus said, 'The time is accomplished and the Kingdom of God is at hand. Repent and believe the gospel.'" (Mark 1:13-15)

FRUIT: EMBRACING JESUS WILL CHANGE THE WORLD

OUR FATHER

"(Jesus) taught them. They were astonished at His doctrine. For He was teaching them as one having power, and not as the scribes." (Mark 1:21-22)
HAIL MARY

"Blessed are the poor in spirit for theirs is the Kingdom of God." (Matthew 5:3)
HAIL MARY

"Blessed are they that suffer persecution for justice sake, for theirs is the Kingdom of Heaven." (Matthew 5:10)
HAIL MARY

"The Kingdom of Heaven is like a treasure that is hidden in a field. A man sells all that he has, with joy, to buy the field." (Matthew 13:44)
HAIL MARY

"The fame of Him spread into all the country of Galilee.
(Jesus) healed many that were troubled with various diseases. And He cast out many devils." (Mark 1:28,34)
HAIL MARY

"So you may know that the Son of Man has power on the earth to forgive sins, I say to you arise take up your bed and go home." (Mark 2:10-11)
HAIL MARY

"Whoever shall not receive the Kingdom of God as a child shall not enter into it." (Mark 10:15)
HAIL MARY

"Do not worry, seek ye first the Kingdom of God and His righteousness." (Matthew 6:33)
HAIL MARY

"The Kingdom of God is within you." (Luke 17:21)
HAIL MARY

"Jesus breathed on them and said, 'Receive the Holy Spirit. Whose sins you shall forgive, they are forgiven them; those sins that you shall retain are retained.'" (John 20:21-22)
HAIL MARY

FOURTH LUMINOUS MYSTERY:
THE TRANSFIGURATION OF CHRIST

"Jesus took with Him Peter and James and John, and led them up a high mountain apart by themselves to pray. (Luke 9:28) Jesus was transfigured before them. And His garments became shining and exceeding white as snow, as no fuller upon earth can make them." (Mark 9:1-2)

FRUIT: CLIMBING THE MOUNTAIN OF LIFE WITH JESUS

OUR FATHER

"Behold two men were talking with Him. And they were Moses and Elijah, appearing in majesty." (Luke 9:30-31)
HAIL MARY

"They spoke of His death that (Jesus) should accomplish in Jerusalem." (Luke 9:31)
HAIL MARY

"Peter said to Jesus: 'Master, it is good for us to be here.'" (Luke 9:33)
HAIL MARY

"Let us make three tabernacles, one for Thee, and one for Moses, and one for Elijah." (Luke 9:33)
HAIL MARY

"He knew not what he said: for they were struck with fear." (Mark 9:5)
HAIL MARY

"There was a cloud overshadowing them. And a voice came out of the cloud, saying: 'This is My most beloved Son. Listen to Him.'" (Mark 9:6)
HAIL MARY

"The disciples hearing the voice, fell...they where very much afraid. Jesus came and touched them and said; 'Arise and fear not.'" (Matthew 17:6-7)
HAIL MARY

"As they came down from the mountain, He charged them not to tell any man what things they had seen, until the Son of man shall rise again from the dead." (Mark 9:8)
HAIL MARY

"They kept the word to themselves; questioning together what Jesus meant by; 'He shall rise from the dead.'" (Mark 9:9)
HAIL MARY

"We all, beholding the glory of the Lord with open face, are transformed into the same image from glory to glory, as by the Spirit of the Lord." (2Corinthians 3:18)
HAIL MARY

FIFTH LUMINOUS MYSTERY:
INSTITUTION OF THE EUCHARIST

"The multitude cried out: "Blessed is He that comes in the name of the Lord. Hosanna in the highest!" (Matthew 21:9)

"They gave (Judas) 30 pieces of silver... Jesus said; 'One of you is about to betray Me.'" (Matthew 26:14-15,21)

"Even a man of My peace, in whom I trusted, who ate My bread, has greatly supplanted Me." (Psalms 41:10)

"As the Father has loved me, I also love you. Live in my Love." (John 15:9)

"Jesus said: 'I give you a new commandment, that you love one another as I have loved you. By this, all men will know that you are My disciples if you have love for one another.'" (Matthew 26:34-35)

FRUIT: ETERNAL UNION WITH GOD

OUR FATHER

"Jesus said: 'Oh, how I desire to eat the Passover with you before I suffer.'" (Luke 22:15)
HAIL MARY

"The Lord said to Moses,'Take a lamb, without blemish, a male... sacrifice it... eat the flesh... I shall see the blood and Pass Over you... and not destroy you."
(Exodus 12:1,5,8,13)
HAIL MARY

"While they were at supper, Jesus took bread, blessed and broke, and gave it to His disciples and said: 'Take and eat; this is My Body.'"
(Matthew 26:26)
HAIL MARY

"Taking a cup He gave thanks and gave it to them saying; 'All of you drink of this. For this is My Blood of the New Covenant, which is being shed for many for the forgiveness of sins.'" (Matthew 26:28); (Jeremiah 31:33)
HAIL MARY

"Jesus said: 'Do this for a commemoration of Me.'"
(Luke 22:19)
HAIL MARY

"Jesus said: 'I am the Bread of life. He that comes to Me shall never hunger, and he that believes in Me shall never thirst.'" (John 6:35)
HAIL MARY

"Jesus said...'He that eats My Flesh and drinks My Blood lives in Me and I in him.'" (John 6:57)
HAIL MARY

"Jesus said; 'This is the Bread that came down from Heaven. Not as your fathers did eat manna and are dead. He that eats this Bread shall live forever.'" (John 6:59)
HAIL MARY

"Jesus said: 'If you keep My commandments, you shall live in My love... My joy may be in you and your joy may be complete.'"
(John 15:10-11)
HAIL MARY

"Father as You are in Me and I in You, I pray that they might be one in Us." (John 17:21)
HAIL MARY

FIRST SORROWFUL MYSTERY:
THE AGONY IN THE GARDEN

"Let nothing hinder you from praying always, and do not be afraid to be justified, even unto death." (Sirach 18:22)

"They gave (Judas) 30 pieces of silver. ...Jesus said 'One of you is about to betray Me.'" (Matthew 26:14-15,21)

"And after reciting a hymn, they went out to Mount Olivet. Then Jesus said to them, 'You will all be scandalized this night because of Me...But after I have risen, I will go before you into Galilee.' But Peter answered and said to Him, 'Even though all shall be scandalized because of Thee, I shall never be scandalized.' Jesus said, 'Amen I say to you, this very night before the cock crows thou will deny Me three times.' Peter said to Him, 'Even if I should have to die with Thee, I will not deny Thee.'" (Matthew 26:26-35)

"Jesus came with them to a country place called Gethsemane, and He said to His disciples, 'Sit down here while I go over yonder and pray.' And He took with Him Peter and the two sons of Zebedee and He began to be saddened and exceedingly troubled. (Jesus) said; 'My soul is sorrowful, even unto death. Stay here and watch.'" (Matthew 26:36-39)

FRUIT OF THE MYSTERY: SORROW FOR SINS

OUR FATHER

"Abba Father, all things are possible to Thee; remove that chalice from Me; but not what I will; but what Thou will." (Mark 14:36)
HAIL MARY

"Then (Jesus) came and found them sleeping. 'Could you not watch one hour?'" (Mark 14:37)
HAIL MARY

"Watch and pray that you enter not into temptation. The spirit is indeed willing, but the flesh is weak." (Mark 14:38)
HAIL MARY

"There appeared to (Jesus) an angel strengthening Him. And He prayed the more earnestly." (Luke 22:43)
HAIL MARY

"He prayed...and his sweat became as drops of blood falling down upon the ground. (Jesus) came to His disciples only to find them asleep." (Luke 22:44-46)
HAIL MARY

"They came with weapons... saying, '(We seek) Jesus of Nazareth!' Jesus replied, 'I AM HE.' Upon hearing, they drew back and fell to the ground." (John 18:4-7); (Exodus 3:14)
HAIL MARY

"'Judas, do you betray the Son of Man with a kiss?'"
(Luke 22:48); (Zacharias 11:12-13); (Matthew 27:3-10)
HAIL MARY

"Simon Peter drew a sword and struck the servant of the high priest and cut off his right ear." (John 18:10)
HAIL MARY

"Jesus said; 'Put away your sword! For all those who take the sword shall perish by the sword.'" (Matthew 26:52)
"Jesus touched his ear and healed him." (Luke 22:51)
HAIL MARY

"All this was done, that the scriptures of the prophets might be fulfilled. Then the disciples all leaving Him, fled." (Matthew 26:56)
"One fled naked." (Mark 14:52); (Amos 2:16)
HAIL MARY

SECOND SORROWFUL MYSTERY:
THE SCOURGING OF JESUS

"Blessed are the clean of heart, for they shall see God."
(Matthew 5:8)
"Follow peace...and holiness: without which no man will see God."
(Hebrews 12:14)
"Now those who had taken Jesus led Him away to Caiphas the high
priest... Peter was following Him at a distance.... Now the chief priests
and all the Sanhedrin were seeking false witness against Jesus, that
they might put Him to death, but they found none...Jesus kept silence."
(Matthew 26:56-63); (Isaiah 53:7)
"They therefore led Jesus from Caiphas to the praetorium. Now it was
early morning, and they themselves did not enter the praetorium, that
they might not be defiled, but might eat the Passover. Pilate therefore
went outside to them, and said, 'What accusation do you bring against
this Man?' They said to him in answer, 'If He were not a criminal
we should not have handed Him over to you.' Pilate therefore said to
them, 'Take Him yourselves, and judge Him according to your law.'
The Jews, then said to him, 'It is not lawful for us to put anyone to
death.'" (John 18:28-31); (Exodus 20:13)

FRUIT OF THE MYSTERY: PURITY

OUR FATHER

"We like sheep have gone astray...and the Lord had laid on Him the
iniquity of us all." (Isaiah 53:6)
HAIL MARY

"Do not err, no fornicator... shall possess the Kingdom of God."
(1Corinthians 6:9-10) "Jesus said; 'Every one who sins is a slave to
sin.'" (John 8:34)
HAIL MARY

"Jesus said, 'You shall know the truth, and the truth shall set you
free.'" (John 8:32) "Everyone who is committed to the truth hears My
voice." (John 18:38)
HAIL MARY

"(Peter) began to curse and swear: 'I do not know this Man you are talking about?' And immediately the cock crowed." (Matthew 26:74)
HAIL MARY

"The Lord turned and looked upon Peter...Peter went out and wept bitterly." (Luke 22:61-62)
HAIL MARY

"The men who had Him in custody began to mock (Jesus) and beat Him." (Luke 22:63); (Isaiah 50:6)
"Then they spat in His face." (Matthew 26:67)
HAIL MARY

"Pilate's next move was to take Jesus and have Him scourged." (John 19:1)
HAIL MARY

"So marred was His look beyond that of man, and His appearance that of mortals." (Isaiah 52:14)
"By His stripes we are healed." (Isaiah 53:5); (1Peter 2:24)
HAIL MARY

"They scourged them...The Apostles rejoiced that they were found worthy to suffer reproach for the Name of Jesus. And continued to preach..." (Acts 5:40-42)
HAIL MARY

"I find my joy in the suffering I endure for you. In my own flesh I fill up what is lacking in the sufferings of Christ for the sake of His Body the Church." (Colossians 1:24)
HAIL MARY

THIRD SORROWFUL MYSTERY:
JESUS IS CROWNED WITH THORNS

"The Kingdom of God is within you." (Luke 17:21)

"Pilate said to Jesus, 'Art thou the king of the Jews? Thy own people and the chief priests have delivered You to me. What have You done?' Jesus answered: 'My kingdom is not of this world.'"
(John 18:28-36)

"The chief priests and the elders persuaded the crowds to ask for Barabbas and to destroy Jesus...Pilate said to them, 'What then am I to do with Jesus who is called Christ?' They all said, 'Let Him be crucified!'..."Why, what evil has He done?' But they kept crying out the more, saying, 'Let Him be crucified!'... 'If thou release this Man, thou art no friend of Caesar; for everyone who makes himself king sets himself against Caesar.'...'Away with Him! Away with Him! Crucify Him!' Pilate said to them, 'Shall I crucify your king?' The chief priests answered, 'We have no king but Caesar.'"
(John 19:12-15)

FRUIT OF THE MYSTERY: COURAGE

OUR FATHER

"Jesus said; 'If someone strikes you on the right cheek, turn and offer him the other.'" (Matthew 5:40)
"They beat Him while others struck His face."
(Matthew 26:67)
HAIL MARY

"They stripped (Jesus) and put on Him a scarlet royal cloak."
(Matthew 27:28)
HAIL MARY

"The soldiers; weaving a crown of thorns put it upon His head and a reed in His right hand." (Matthew 27:29)
HAIL MARY

"Abraham said; 'God himself will provide a victim for the sacrifice'....
Then he saw a Ram with his head caught in thorns."
(Genesis 22:8,13)
HAIL MARY

"Behold the Man!" (John 19:6); (Isaiah 53:3)
HAIL MARY

"And bending the knee before (Jesus) they mocked Him saying, 'Hail,
king of the Jews!'" (Matthew 27:29)
HAIL MARY

"We are tired of this wretched (bread)!" (Numbers 11:6,21:5);
"And they spat on Him, and took the reed and kept striking Him on the
head." (Matthew 27:30)
HAIL MARY

"Behold your King!" (John 19:15)
"Thy Kingdom come, Thy will be done." (Matthew 6:10)
HAIL MARY

"Lord of Lords and King of Kings." (Revelations 17:14)
"Of His Kingdom there shall be no end." (Luke 1:33)
HAIL MARY

"God is King of all the earth." (Psalms 47: 7-8)
"All the kings of the earth shall adore Him...all nations shall serve
Him." (Psalms 72:11); (Rev 21:23-24)
HAIL MARY

FOURTH SORROWFUL MYSTERY:
JESUS CARRIES THE CROSS

"Blessed are they that hunger and thirst after justice."
(Matthew 5:6)

"Pilate said to (Jesus), 'Don't you know I have the power to crucify You, and I have the power to release You?' Jesus answered, 'You would not have any power over Me whatsoever, unless it was given to you from above. Therefore, he that delivered Me to you has the greater sin.' Pilate sought to release (Jesus)." (John 19:10-12)
"But they all cried, 'Let Him be crucified.' Now Pilate, seeing that he was doing no good, but rather that a riot was breaking out, took water and washed his hands, saying, 'I am innocent of the blood of this just Man; see to it yourselves.' And all the people answered, 'His blood be on us and on our children.'" (Matthew 27:23-25)

FRUIT OF THE MYSTERY: PATIENCE

OUR FATHER

"I Am the Way, the Truth and the Life." (John 14:6)
HAIL MARY

"'Whoever wishes to come after Me must deny himself, take up his cross and follow Me...For what does it profit a man to gain the whole world, but lose his soul?'"
(Matthew 16:24,26)
HAIL MARY

"'Behold the lamb of God, Who takes away the sin of the world."
(John 1:29)
HAIL MARY

"He laid the wood on Isaac his son...they went up the mountain."
(Genesis 22:6)
HAIL MARY

"They forced a man named Simon of Cyrene to take up His Cross. They came to a place called Golgotha, that is, the place of the skull." (Matthew 27:33)
HAIL MARY

"He humbled Himself, becoming obedient unto death, even to death on the Cross. For which God also has exalted Him and has given Him a name which is above all names." (Philippians 2:8,9)
HAIL MARY

"That in the name of Jesus, every knee should bend and every tongue shall confess, to the glory of God the Father, that Jesus Christ is Lord." (Philippians 2:10-11); (Isaiah 45:22-25)
HAIL MARY

"'Daughters of Jerusalem weep not for Me, but weep for yourselves and for your children. For if these things happen when the wood is green, what will happen when it is dry?'" (Luke 23:28,31)
HAIL MARY

"Be followers of me, brethren...for many who walk are enemies of the Cross of Christ." (Philippians 3:18)
HAIL MARY

"Christ sent me to preach the Gospel. Not in wisdom of speech or else the Cross of Christ would lose its power." (1Corinthians 1:17); (Gal 6:14)
HAIL MARY

FIFTH SORROWFUL MYSTERY:
THE CRUCIFIXION OF JESUS

"With Christ, I am nailed to the Cross. It is no longer I that live, but Christ lives in me." (Galations 2:19-20)

"No one has greater love than this: to lay down ones life for ones friends." (John 15:13); (Galations 3:13)

"They crucified Him...They put over His head the cause written; 'THIS IS THE KING OF THE JEWS'... They that passed by, blasphemed Him, wagging their heads, saying, 'You that will destroy the temple and in three days rebuild it, save Thyself, if Thou art the Son of God, come down from the Cross.' The chief priests with the scribes mockingly said; 'He saved others but Himself He cannot save! If He be the King of Israel, let Him now come down from the Cross, and we will believe Him.'"

(Matthew 27:35-42); (Wisdom 2:18)

"Jesus said; "When you lift up the Son of Man, you shall know that I Am He."(John 8:28); (Ezekiel 37:12-14)

FRUIT OF THE MYSTERY: PERSEVERANCE

OUR FATHER

"Love one another, as I have loved you." (John 13:34)
HAIL MARY

"They have pierced my hands and my feet. They divided my garments amongst them and upon my vestures they cast lots."
(Psalms 22:17-19); (Acts 5:30); (Zecharia 13:6-7)
HAIL MARY

"Love your enemies. Pray for those who persecute you."
(Matthew 5:44)
"Father forgive them, for they do not know what they are doing."
(Luke 23:34)
HAIL MARY

"'Lord remember me when You come into Your kingdom.' And Jesus said; 'Amen I say to you, this day you will be with Me in paradise.'"
(Luke 23:42-43)
HAIL MARY

"Jesus said to His mother, 'Woman behold thy son' and to the disciple
He said, 'Behold thy Mother.' After that he took Her into his home."
(John 19:27); (Psalms 87); (Galatians 4:26)
HAIL MARY

"'My God, My God, why has thou abandoned Me?'"
(Matthew 27:47); (Psalms 22:1)
"A man shall leave his father and mother and cleave to his wife and the
two shall become one flesh. This is a great sacrament. In Christ and
the Church." (Ephesians 5:31-32); (Genesis 2:24)
HAIL MARY

"I thirst...it is finished." (John 19:28,30); (Psalms 69:22) "'Father into
Thy hands, I commend My Spirit.' Upon saying this (Jesus died)."
(Luke 23:46); (Psalms 31:6)
HAIL MARY

"His side was pierced with a lance, immediately, blood and water
flowed forth." (John 19:34); (Zechariah 12:10);
(Revelations 1:5); (Genesis 2:21-23); (Hebrews 9)
HAIL MARY

"There was darkness over the whole earth. The curtain of the temple
was torn into two and the earth quaked. Many bodies of Saints arose.
The centurion said, 'Truly this Man is the Son of God.'"
(Matthew 27:47,51,54)
HAIL MARY

"We preach Christ crucified, a stumbling block to the Jews and foolish-
ness to the Gentiles...but Christ is the power and the wisdom of God."
(1Corinthians 1:23-24)
HAIL MARY

THE FIRST GLORIOUS MYSTERY:
THE RESURRECTION OF JESUS

"Blessed are the merciful: for they shall obtain mercy."
(Matthew 5:7)

"Jesus said; 'Destroy this temple...in three days I will raise it up.'"
(John 2:19); (Jonas 2:1)

"When it began to dawn towards the first day of the week, came Mary
Magdalene and the other Mary, to see the sepulcher. And behold, there
was a great earthquake. For an angel of the Lord descended from
heaven, and coming, rolled back the stone and sat upon it. And for fear
of him, the guards were struck with terror and became as dead men.
The angel said to the women: 'Fear not, for I know you seek Jesus
who was crucified. He is not here, for He has risen as He said.
Come and see the place where they laid Him.'"
(Matthew 28:1-7); (Zephaniah 3:8)

FRUIT OF THE MYSTERY: FAITH

OUR FATHER

"Christ, having risen from the dead, will never die again, death has
no power over Him. You must die to sin, be alive for God in Jesus
Christ." (Romans 6:9-11)
HAIL MARY

"The angel said to Mary Magdalene, 'Go, tell His disciples and Peter
that He goes before you to Galilee; there you shall see Him, as He
said.'" (Mark 16:7)
HAIL MARY

"Peter and the other disciple ran together to the sepulcher and saw the
linen cloths lying there. The other disciple saw, and believed."
(John 20:4-8)
HAIL MARY

"(Thomas) said to them, 'unless I shall see the print of the nails and put my hand into His side, I will not believe.'" (John 20:25)
HAIL MARY

"Jesus came, though the doors were locked and said, 'Peace be to you. Thomas, put your finger in My hands, and put your hand into My side, and be not faithless but believe.'" (John 20:27)
HAIL MARY

"Thomas replied; 'My Lord and my God.'" (John 20:28)
HAIL MARY

"Jesus said, 'Blessed are they that have not seen, and have believed.'" (John 20:29)
HAIL MARY

"They knew (Jesus) in the breaking of the bread." (Luke 24:35)
HAIL MARY

"Just as in Adam all die, so also in Christ all will come to life." (1Corinthians 15:22); (Romans 5:9-21)
HAIL MARY

"Jesus did many other signs. These are written, that you may believe that Jesus is the Christ, the Son of God and that believing, you may have life in His name." (John 20:30-31)
HAIL MARY

SECOND GLORIOUS MYSTERY:
ASCENSION OF JESUS INTO HEAVEN

"You shall see the Son of Man sitting on the right hand of the power of God." (Matthew 26:64)
"For forty days Jesus appeared to them and spoke of the kingdom of God." (Acts 1:3)

"Jesus said; 'Go into the whole world and preach the Gospel to every creature. He that believes and is baptized shall be saved, but he that believes not, shall be condemned...In My name they shall cast out devils...speak with new tongues...take up serpents...and if they shall drink any deadly thing, it shall not hurt them. They shall lay their hands upon the sick, and they shall recover."
(Mark 16:15-18); (Ezechiel 36:25-28)

FRUIT OF THE MYSTERY: HOPE

OUR FATHER

"Then (Jesus) opened their understanding, that they might understand the scriptures...Jesus said; 'Preach penance and remission of sins, in His Name, to all nations.'" (Luke 24:46-47)
HAIL MARY

"As the Father has sent Me, I also sent you." (John 20:21) "I am the Vine, you are the branches...He that lives in Me and I in him, will bear much fruit." (John 15:5); (Revelations 22:2); (Psalm 80)
HAIL MARY

"(Jesus) breathed on them and said: 'Receive the Holy Ghost, whose sins you shall forgive, they are forgiven, those you retain, they are retained.'" (John 20:22-23); (Genesis 2:7)
HAIL MARY

"Simon Peter, son of John, do you love Me?...Feed My sheep." (John 21:17); (John 10:14-16); (Psalm 23:1-2)
HAIL MARY

"Jesus said...'Thou art Peter; and upon this rock I will build My Church, and the gates of hell shall not prevail against it...I will give thee the keys of the Kingdom of Heaven, and whatever you shall bind on earth, it shall be bound also in heaven."
(Matthew 16:18-19); (Isaiah 22:10)
HAIL MARY

"All power is given to Me in Heaven and earth...Teach them to observe all things whatsoever I commanded you: and behold I am with you all days, even to the end of the world."
(Matthew 28:18-20)
HAIL MARY

"I send the promise of My Father upon you: but stay in the city, until you receive power from upon High." (Luke 24:49)
HAIL MARY

"'(Jesus) was raised up: and a cloud received Him out of their sight....' (The Angel) said 'This Jesus...will come again, as you seen Him going to Heaven.'" (Acts 1:9-11); (2 Kings 2:1-15)
HAIL MARY

"They preached everywhere: the Lord worked with them, and confirming the Word with signs that followed."
(Mark 16:20); (1 Timothy 3:16)
HAIL MARY

"Rejoice always! Pray without ceasing! In all things give thanks... Do not extinguish the Spirit...do not despise prophecy. Test all things, hold fast to what is good."
(1 Thessalonians 5:16-21)
HAIL MARY

THIRD GLORIOUS MYSTERY:
THE DESCENT OF THE HOLY SPIRIT

"I will not leave you orphans...The Paraclete, the Holy Spirit, whom
the Father will send in My name, He will teach you all things."
(John 14:18,26)
"The Spirit of Wisdom, Understanding, Counsel, Fortitude, Knowledge, Piety, Fear of the Lord." (Isaiah 11:2-3)
"They were persevering with one mind in prayer with the women,
and Mary the Mother of Jesus, and with His brethren." (Acts 1:14)
"And when the days of Pentecost were accomplished...there came a
sound from Heaven, as of a mighty wind, and it filled the whole house
where they were sitting. And there appeared to them parted tongues
of fire, and it sat upon every one of them: And they were all filled with
the Holy Ghost, and they began to speak with foreign tongues....The
multitude came together and were confounded in mind because every
man heard them speak in his own tongue."
(Acts 2:1-6)

FRUIT OF THE MYSTERY : LOVE OF GOD

OUR FATHER

"Jesus said: 'When the Spirit of Truth comes...He shall glorify Me
because He will take what is Mine and reveal it to you.'"
(John 16:13,14)
HAIL MARY

"Peter standing up said...'It shall come to pass, in the last days, says
the Lord, I will pour out of My Spirit upon all flesh.'"
(Acts 2:17); (Joel 2:28)
HAIL MARY

"Your sons and daughters shall prophesy...your young men shall see
visions. I will show wonders in the Heavens above and signs on the
earth." (Acts 2:19)
HAIL MARY

"God raised Jesus again, and we are His witnesses...God has made both Lord and Christ this Jesus whom you have crucified."
(Acts 2:32,36); (Galations 3:13)
HAIL MARY

"Do penance, and be baptized every one of you in the name of Jesus Christ, for the remission of your sins: and you will receive the Holy Ghost." (Acts 2:38); (Exod 14:29)
HAIL MARY

"'Save yourself from this perverse generation...' And there were added that day about three thousand souls."
(Acts 2:40,41); (1Peter 3:20-21)
HAIL MARY

"They were persevering in the doctrine of the apostles, and in the communication of the breaking of bread and in prayers." (Acts 2:42)
"As they prayed, the (walls) shook...all were filled with the Holy Spirit." (Acts 4:31)
HAIL MARY

"If this work is from men, it will fail. If it is from God, you will not be able to stop it, else you will be even fighting God."
(Acts 5:38-39); (Psalm 130:30); (Num 11:25)
HAIL MARY

"Your body is the temple of the Holy Spirit, Who is in you...for you have been bought at a great price. Glorify God and bear Him in your body." (1Cor 6:19-20)
HAIL MARY

"If anyone thirst, let him come to Me and drink...from within him, there shall flow rivers of living water." (John 7:37-38)
"The fruit of the Spirit is Love, Joy, Peace, Patience, Kindness, Faith... and Chastity." (Galatians 5:22)
HAIL MARY

THE FOURTH GLORIOUS MYSTERY:
ASSUMPTION OF THE BLESSED VIRGIN MARY

"All generations shall call Me blessed." (Luke 1:48)
"Jesus said; 'Build up for yourself treasure in Heaven.'"
(Matthew 6:20)
"In the end, three things last; Faith, Hope and Love and the greatest of
these is Love." (1Corinthians 13:13)
"Jesus said..."Thou shall love the Lord thy God with your whole heart,
whole soul, and whole mind. This is the greatest and the first com-
mandment.'" (Matthew 22:37)
"Arise, make haste, my love, my dove, my beautiful one and come...
Thou art all fair, o my love, and there is not a spot in thee."
(Songs 2:10, 3:7)
"Rejoice...and be glad...all you that love Her! Rejoice for joy...all you
that mourn for Her...Behold I will bring upon her as it were a river of
peace." (Isaiah 66:10,12)

FRUIT OF THE MYSTERY: GRACE OF A HAPPY DEATH

OUR FATHER

"Eye has not seen, nor ear heard, neither has it entered into the heart of
man, what things God has prepared for them that love Him."
(1 Corinthians 2:9); (Isaiah 64:4)
HAIL MARY

"Whoever eats My Flesh, and drinks My Blood, has everlasting life:
and I will raise them up on the last day." (John 6:55)
HAIL MARY

"All good things came to me together with Her, and innumerable
riches through Her hands...the Mother of them all...an infinite treasure
to men." (Wisdom 7:11-14)
HAIL MARY

"In the midst of her own people she shall be exalted, and shall be
admired in the holy assembly." (Sirach 24:3)
HAIL MARY

"Come to Me all you that yearn for me." (Sirach 24:18)
"I will yet pour out doctrine as prophecy, and will leave it to them that
seek wisdom." (Sirach 24:18, 46)
HAIL MARY

"Mary said...'Do whatever (Jesus) tells you.'" (John 2:5)
"Jesus said, 'Whoever does and teaches others (to keep My command-
ments) shall be called great in the Kingdom of Heaven.'"
(Matthew 5:19)
HAIL MARY

"She is an aura of the might of God... the spotless mirror of the power
of God, and the image of His goodness... And passing into holy souls
She makes the friends of God and prophets."
(Wisdom 7:25,26,27); (Psalm 44:14)
HAIL MARY

"Her ways are beautiful ways, and all Her paths are peace. She is a
tree of life to them that lay hold of Her: he that retains Her is blessed."
(Proverbs 3:17-18)*
HAIL MARY

"You are a garden enclosed." (Songs 4:12); (Matthew 13:23)
"You are the splendid boast of our people, God is pleased, may you be
blessed by the Lord almighty forever and ever." (Judith 15:9-10)
HAIL MARY

"In My Father's house there are many mansions...I go to prepare a
place for you...I will come again and take you to Myself."
(Jn 14:2-3) "The Spirit and the bride say come...and let him that is
thirsty come...and let him take the water of life freely."
(Revelation 22:17)
HAIL MARY

FIFTH GLORIOUS MYSTERY:
THE CORONATION OF THE BLESSED MOTHER
AS QUEEN OF HEAVEN.

"He that's mighty has done great things to Me." (Luke 1:49) "The queen stood on thy right hand, clothed in gold...the king shall greatly desire thy beauty; for He is the Lord thy God."
(Psalms 45:9,12); (1 Kings 2:19)

"Who is She that comes forth as the morning rising, fair as the moon, bright as the sun, as terrible as an army set in battle array."
(Songs 6:10); (2Paralipom 20:15)

"Jesus said 'Behold thy Mother.'" (John 19:17,27); (Ps 87) "Behold a great sign appeared in heaven: a Woman clothed with the sun, and the moon under Her feet, and on Her head a crown of twelve stars. And being with child, She cried...and was in pain to be delivered."
(Revelation 12:1,2)

FRUIT: TRUST IN MARY'S INTERCESSION

OUR FATHER

"My little children, of whom I am in labor again until Christ be formed in you." (Galations 4:19); (Genesis 3:20)
HAIL MARY

"We are many members of one Body. The Body of Christ."
(1Corinthians 12:20,27) "Christ is the head of the Church. (Jesus) is the Savior of His Body." (Ephesians 5:23)
HAIL MARY

"God said to the serpent, 'I will put enmities between you and the Woman and your seed and Her seed. She shall crush your head and you shall lie in wait of Her heel.'" (Genesis 3:14-15)
HAIL MARY

"And there was a great battle in heaven, Michael and his angels fought with the dragon...That old serpent who is the Devil and Satan."
(Revelation 12:7,9); (Daniel 12:1); (Daniel 10:21)
HAIL MARY

"The (Devil) persecuted the Woman...The serpent cast out of his mouth, water as a flood after the Woman. That he might cause Her to be carried away." (Rev 12:13,15)
HAIL MARY

"The earth helped Her" (Revelations 12:16) "Many waters cannot quench love, neither can the floods drown it."
(Songs 8:7) "Only prayer and fasting can drive out this demon."
(Matthew 17:20); (Jonas 3:5); (Joel 1:14-15)
HAIL MARY

"The dragon was angry against the Woman: and went to make war with the rest of Her seed, who keep the commandments of God, and have the testimony of Jesus Christ."
(Rev 12:17); (Romans 13:11-14); (Ephes 6:11-12)
HAIL MARY

"Blessed are they that suffer persecution for justice sake, for theirs is the Kingdom of Heaven." (Matthew 5:10) "I fought the good fight, I kept the faith, a glorious crown awaits me."
(2Timothy 4:7); (1Cor 9:24-27); (Daniel 8:11)
HAIL MARY

"The Lamb will conquer!"
(Samuel 17:50); (Revelations 1:5, 17:14, 22:14)
"Receive the crown of life, which God has promised to them that love Him." (James 1:12)
HAIL MARY

"The king will say to those on his right hand; 'Come, blessed of My Father, take possession of the kingdom prepared for you from the foundation of the world.'"
(Matthew 25:34); (Psalms 45:17); (Romans 8:17)
HAIL MARY

THE ROSARY WEAPON
BATTLE PLAN

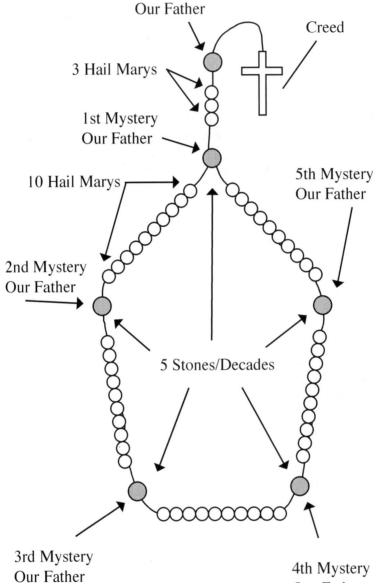

CHAPTER TWENTY
- THE PRAYERS

THE 'APOSTLES' CREED

I believe in God, the Father almighty, creator of heaven and earth and in Jesus Christ, his only son, our Lord. Who was conceived by the Holy Spirit, born of the Virgin Mary. He suffered under Pontius Pilate, was crucified, died, and was buried. He descended to the dead. On the third day He rose again from the dead. He ascended into heaven, and is seated at the right hand of God the Father almighty. From there He will come to judge the living and the dead. I believe in the Holy Spirit, the holy Catholic Church, the communion of saints, the forgiveness of sins, the resurrection of the body, and life everlasting. Amen.

THE OUR FATHER

Our Father, Who art in Heaven; hallowed be Thy name; Thy Kingdom come, Thy will be done on earth as it is in Heaven. Give us this day our daily bread; and forgive us our trespasses as we forgive those who trespass against us, and lead us not into temptation, but deliver us from evil. Amen.

THREE HAIL MARYS (for Faith, Hope and Love)
Hail Mary, full of grace, the Lord is with Thee; blessed art Thou among women, and blessed is the fruit of Thy womb, Jesus. Holy Mary, Mother of God, pray for us sinners, now and at the hour of our death. Amen.

GLORY BE
Glory Be to the Father, and to the Son, and to the Holy Spirit. As it was in the beginning, is now, and will be forever. Amen.

BETWEEN EACH DECADE
Oh my Jesus, forgive us our sins, save us from the fires of hell, lead all souls to Heaven, especially those who have most need of Your mercy.

HAIL, HOLY QUEEN
Hail, Holy Queen, Mother of Mercy, our life, our sweetness and our hope, to You do we cry, poor banished children of Eve; to You do we send up our sighs, mourning and weeping in this valley of tears; turn, then, most gracious Advocate, Your eyes of mercy towards us, and after this, our exile, show unto us the blessed fruit of Your womb, Jesus. O Clement, O Loving, O Sweet Virgin Mary! Pray for us, O holy Mother of God, that we may be made worthy of the promises of Christ.

ST. MICHAEL
St. Michael the Archangel, defend us in battle; Be our safeguard against the wickedness and snares of the Devil. May God rebuke him, we humbly pray, and do Thou, O Prince of the Heavenly Host, by the Divine power of God, thrust into Hell, Satan and all the evil spirits, who wander throughout the world, seeking the ruin of souls. Amen.

MEMORARE
Remember O Most Gracious Virgin Mary, that never was it known, that anyone who fled to Thy protection, implored Thy help or sought Thy intercession was left unaided. Inspired by this confidence I fly unto Thee, O Virgin of virgins my Mother. To Thee I come, before Thee I stand sinful and sorrowful. O Mother of the Word Incarnate, despise not my petitions, but in Thy mercy hear and answer me. Amen.

15 Promises from Heaven, delivered by Our Lady to Saint Dominic and Blessed Alan O.P.

1. Whoever shall faithfully serve Me by the recitation of the Rosary shall receive special graces.

2. I promise my special protection and the greatest graces to all those who shall recite the Rosary.

3. The Rosary shall be a powerful armor against hell. It will destroy vice, decrease sin, and defeat heresy.

4. It will cause virtue and good works to flourish. It will obtain for souls the abundant mercy of God. It will withdraw the hearts of men from the love of the world and its vanities and will lift them to the desire of eternal things. Oh, that souls would sanctify themselves by this means!

5. The soul that recommends itself to Me by the recitation of the Rosary shall not perish.

6. Whoever shall recite the Rosary devoutly, applying himself to the consideration of its sacred mysteries shall never be conquered by misfortune. If he be a sinner, he shall not perish by an unprovided death. If he be just, he shall remain in the grace of God. He shall become worthy of eternal life.

7. Whoever shall have a true devotion for the Rosary shall not die without the sacraments of the Church.

8. Those who are faithful to the recitation of the Rosary shall have during their life and at their death the light of God and the plenitude of His graces at the moment of death. They shall participate in the merits of the saints in paradise.

9. I shall deliver from purgatory those who have been devoted to the Rosary.

10. The faithful children of the Rosary shall merit a high degree of glory in heaven.

11. You shall obtain all you ask of Me by the recitation of the Rosary.

12. All those who propagate the holy Rosary shall be aided by Me in their necessities.

13. I have obtained from my divine Son that all the advocates of the Rosary shall have for intercessors the entire celestial court during their life and at the hour of death.

14. All who recite the Rosary are My sons and daughters, and brothers and sisters of my Son, Jesus Christ.

15. Devotion to My Rosary is a great sign of predestination.

St. James Church, Medjugorje

If this work is from men, it will fail.
If it is from God, you will not be able to stop it,
else you will be even fighting God.

(Acts 5:38-39)

The Lord God said to the serpent (devil).....
"I will put enmities between you and the Woman-
between your seed and her seed.
She shall crush your head while you lie in wait of her heel."

(Genesis 3:15)

The statue of the Blessed Virgin Mary is located in front of
St. James Church at Medjugorje.

The dragon (devil) was angry against the Woman
and went to make war with the rest of her seed
who keep the commandments of God and have the
testimony of Jesus Christ.

(Revelations 12:17)

ORDER INFORMATION

Help us evangelize Our Lady's Message to the Spiritually hungry souls.

The Weapon of Medjugorje Full Size $14.95, see inside front
cover. A true story of an engineer who challenged Our Lady of Medjugorje and discovered the true weapon.

The Weapon of Medjugorje Pocket Size Version:

$5⁰⁰ Add $3.⁰⁰ S & H (shipping & handling)
5 for $20⁰⁰ Add $4.⁰⁰ S & H
10 for $35⁰⁰ Add $5.⁰⁰ S & H
Case of 50 for $150⁰⁰ Add $7.⁰⁰ S & H

Angels of the Last Days - Teach Your Soul How To Fly In 33 Days
The Angels will help you to learn how to meditate so you can direct your pilgrimage on earth to reach heaven.

$5⁰⁰ Add $3.⁰⁰ S & H (shipping & handling)
5 for $20⁰⁰ Add $4.⁰⁰ S & H
10 for $35⁰⁰ Add $5.⁰⁰ S & H
Case of 50 for $150⁰⁰ Add $7.⁰⁰ S & H

Our Lady of the Cross
Messages given to Joe Reinholtz at Queen of Heaven Cemetary, Hillside IL.

$3⁰⁰ Add $3.⁰⁰ S & H (shipping & handling)
10 for $25⁰⁰ Add $4.⁰⁰ S & H
Case of 50 for $100⁰⁰ Add $7.⁰⁰ S & H

Proceeds go to help build a youth retreat center for The Sacred Heart Center for Peace

Not-for-profit (501 C 3)

Make checks payable to: Sacred Heart Center for Peace
P.O. Box 927
Wilmette, IL 60091

RELATED WEB SITES

www.medj1.com